Sin and Madness

Sin and Madness:
Studies in Narcissism

by

SHIRLEY SUGERMAN

THE WESTMINSTER PRESS
Philadelphia

COPYRIGHT © 1976 THE WESTMINSTER PRESS

art of this book may be repro-
ut permission in writing from
ı reviewer who wishes to quote
ion with a review in magazine

IGN BY DOROTHY ALDEN SMITH

Published by The Westminster Press ®
Philadelphia, Pennsylvania

PRINTED IN THE UNITED STATES OF AMERICA

Library of Congress Cataloging in Publication Data

Sugerman, Shirley.
  Sin and madness.

  Bibliography: p.
  Includes index.
  1. Narcissism. 2. Psychology, Pathological.
3. Sin—Psychology. 4. East and West. I. Title.
BF575.N35S84   157   76–26033
ISBN 0–664–24125–5

Narcissism presents itself to us no longer only as a type of sexual deviation or only as the description of a neurosis, but as a major spiritual aberration running through the whole history of mankind, going back as long as we have records and spreading everywhere man has set up his dwelling.

Grace Stuart, Narcissus

Contents

Preface

> Man . . . has plainly gone astray, and fallen from his true place
> without being able to find it again. He seeks it anxiously and
> unsuccessfully everywhere in impenetrable darkness.
>
> *Blaise Pascal*[1]

> Alienation as our present destiny is achieved only by outrageous
> violence perpetrated by human beings on human beings.
>
> *R. D. Laing*[2]

OURS IS A TIME in which the madness of man has become
glaringly apparent. It has become intensified to the point
where Pascal's *pensée* seems written for a contemporary journal rather than a seventeenth-century notebook. Pascal is in
fact echoed and specified by Laing's contemporary comment
on the predicament. Our very seeking, our "strategies for survival," seem paradoxically to be leading us deeper into division
and closer to self-destruction. The gulf between our acknowledged and unacknowledged intentions has widened, revealing
so dark and deep a chasm that we are shocked into taking
notice. These disjunct intentions have split us in two. We find
ourselves, seemingly unwittingly, going in opposite directions.
We preach love and do violence. We speak of peace and make
war. We praise "progress" and sense doom. We are indeed
divided selves in a divided world. The demonic course that man
has been on for well over twenty centuries seems to be leading
not only to suicide but also to ecocide. What has *prevented* us
from reversing our course? Why have our apparently "good
intentions" generated the opposite results? We have been
taught through the ages what the "good" is, and even how to

11

do "the good," but we haven't discovered what our resistance is to following those teachings. This concern with the patterns of human behavior and the need for self-understanding consistent with traditional wisdom, and yet congenial to the modern consciousness, has led to this book.

Of course, our malaise has been under scrutiny for quite some time. Hegel, Kierkegaard, Marx, Nietzsche, Freud—to suggest only a few names of the modern era—have found one thing or another wrong with the human condition. Strangely, little or no attention has been given to these diagnoses and we have moved ever deeper into our madness. One wonders whether there is, as Robert Heilbroner has suggested, "the [unacknowledged] wish that the human drama run its full tragic course [and] bring man like a Greek hero to the fearful end that he has, however unwittingly, arranged for himself."[3]

My reason for presenting my analysis of our situation is that studies in the self have led me to an understanding of sin, as it is traditionally defined, and madness, in a more contemporary idiom, as correlative modes that reflect the human situation in a similar way. Later Eastern studies suggested images of man that relate to and reflect a similar understanding of the human condition and of man's existential relationship to being —granting, of course, cultural differences. Furthermore, psychoanalytic work and studies over a long period of time led to the practical, concrete, and specific understanding of our condition as narcissism, as well as to the therapeutic possibilities inherent in that understanding. Finally, all the paths that I followed in my search for understanding led to the image of Narcissus as the metaphor of the human condition but not the myth of Narcissus as it is usually interpreted as a representation of self-love. My awareness of these deep connections and my desire to put all the strands of this skein together, despite the obvious difficulties involved in cross-cultural and cross-disciplinary correlations, have resulted in this volume. Convinced of the core of human reality underlying the complexities, as well as the need for an informative pattern that would bring some order out of the chaotic multitude of "facts" with which we are confronted, I have risked making the generalizations requisite to that task. What has emerged, I hope, is a mirror in which we can catch ourselves in midcourse and gaze long enough to understand and perhaps, with what freedom we have, even begin to remedy what seems to be our fate. It is the fate of all of us, not only of those considered "pathological." To some degree, everyman is Narcissus. If we continue to make war for the sake of peace, if we continue to do violence with our love on any level of human relationships, individual *or* communal, the survival of man is endangered.

It is not possible to record all who have helped with this book. But I would like to acknowledge my gratitude to Will Herberg, for his initial encouragement to undertake this work; to Owen Barfield, for his detailed comments and perceptive questions; to Hyman Spotnitz, for his insight into the intention of the book, and his helpful suggestions. I also want to thank Charles Courtney, Sidney Greenblatt, John Ollom, James Pain, and Roger Wescott, who read the manuscript in various stages and were generous with their time and comments. My thanks also to the students in my classes in world religions whose questions made me think harder than I might have. For editorial assistance, I am grateful to Carol Rothkopf; for assistance with references, to Jaia Heyman and Louise Capron of the Drew University library; for her faithfulness at the typewriter, to Chia Whitehouse. And since the last shall be first, I have waited until now to express my appreciation to my husband, Morton Rosenberg, for his cooperation and his willingness to share our life with the writing of this book.

Chapter 4, "Sin and Madness: A Transformation of Consciousness," is a revision of my article in *The Psychoanalytic Review*, Vol LXI, No. 4 (1974–75). It is used here through the courtesy of the Editors and the Publisher, National Psychological Association for Psychoanalysis, New York, N.Y.

S.S.

Drew University
Madison, New Jersey

1
Narcissus Reconsidered: The Myth

> I know the truth at last. He is myself! I feel it, I know my image now. I burn with love of my own self! I start the fire I suffer.
>
> *Ovid* [1]

> Since man has lost the true good everything can appear equally good to him, even his own destruction.
>
> *Blaise Pascal* [2]

MERELY TO DIAGNOSE the acute schizophrenia of the human spirit or to be an archaeologist of its ruins is insufficient. What we need is a revision of our long-standing, but now crumbling, self-image. We need a model for self-understanding in the post-Freudian era. To achieve this goal we must take a look at our fundamental relationship to ourselves, to others, and to existence itself. From what perspective can we explore this vast arena? How can we understand our relationship to ourselves and others? In what image is that relationship, and hence our portrait, best reflected? My answer is the image of Narcissus, the myth that deals with reflections and, indeed, with far, far more than that, when the whole tale is told. For it is the myth of Narcissus that mirrors back to us our strange condition and emerges ultimately as an extraordinary metaphor for the human situation.

Our predicament is not new. The ancient wisdom of both East and West had told repeatedly of man's tendency to self-idolatry, self-encapsulation, and its result: self-destruction. Self-worship—pride—is fatal. But why? Why the tendency and why the fatality? It is this question which the myth of Narcissus illuminates. It suggests that there is a fate for us that is *worse* than death and that it is against this fate that we seek to defend ourselves, paradoxically with the very armor that defeats us. Self-worship is a defensive maneuver against the fateful perception of man's lovelessness and rejection and against the recognition of the murderous rage provoked. Self-absorption is then a strategy for survival in the face of this condition, but it is a strategy that inevitably fails—as all traditions, Eastern and Western, warn us. Self-worship serves only to mask and disguise this condition—this fate worse than death—about which we have wanted to know nothing. In fact, we have been forewarned repeatedly not to seek such knowledge. The Greek axiom "Know thyself" has been countered by the warning of the legendary Greek seer Tiresias that such knowledge is fatal. In Genesis (ch. 3:3–12) we are admonished not to partake of the tree of knowledge—to "become as gods"—which carries the implicit threat of death. But now, so corrosive is the masked condition, so destructive the unacknowledged inner forces, and so tragic a failure the strategy, that we must make the wager and risk self-understanding.

Unable simply to "return" to our original condition, to set it right, we need to find a way to touch ancient bases. One of the primary ways to understand the being of man is through the symbolism of the eternally repeated myths. I see the task as Paul Ricoeur states it: "to break out of the enchanted enclosure of consciousness of oneself"[3] and, "starting from symbols, to elaborate existential concepts."[4] By interpretation of the myth, the symbol's "gift of meaning" may be released so that we can "hear" again. The traditional symbols, traditionally understood, are not speaking to us.

The myths that used to inform us seem no longer viable. The possible forms of our understanding have changed. Two fundamental strands of Western culture have disintegrated. The Biblical understanding of man as *imago Dei* has been called into question, as well as the traditional Greek belief in the correspondence between rationality and reality, and in man as rational being. We have lost two major ways of understanding ourselves. Referring to the traditional Biblical view of man in the image of God, the German philosopher Friedrich Nietzsche wrote that "to have lost God means madness; and when mankind will discover that it has lost God, universal madness will break out."[5] According to R. D. Laing, the Scottish psychiatrist, man's radical estrangement from his Source and idolatry of his own self, the "absence of presence," also means madness. *"Deus Absconditus.* Or we have absconded." Therefore "we are in an age of darkness. The state of outer darkness is the state of sin—that is, alienation or estrangement from the inner light."[6]

This estrangement of inner and outer worlds and the resulting self-encapsulation is madness. It used to be understood as sin. In the tradition of theology following Augustine, in which Kierkegaard is located, sin is viewed as self-glorification and man's estrangement from his Source—the opposite of faith. The self becomes an end unto itself. Luther understood sin as the self-enclosed self, one curved back on itself *(incurvatum in se).*[7] Pascal wrote that "self is hateful . . . because it makes itself the center of everything. . . . It is . . . the enemy and would . . . be the tyrant of all others."[8] He says that "men are so necessarily mad, that not to be mad would amount to another form of madness."[9] Man has gone "astray," is separated from his Source, and seeks his "true place in impenetrable darkness."[10] The symbolism of sin in the Biblical tradition suggests a disruption in man's relationship to God as Other. Sin is the rejection of grace and the worship of false gods, which is nothingness, and which means nonbeing, death, for man.

Although *imago Dei,* the old mythos, may no longer be viable, there is now a view of madness that suggests that the old doctrine exists but is expressed in a different form. It understands madness not as disease, but as the equivalent of sin—a disorder of the spirit—a disruption of man's fundamental relationship to existence. This "sickness of the spirit . . . threatens mankind with death."[11]

It is becoming clear that just such a new interpretation of the old mythos has indeed been emerging to heighten our self-understanding. Instead of the traditional terms of sin and faith, the alternatives now are sanity and madness. Although not equivalents, the polarity sanity/madness seems to be replacing that of faith/sin. Indeed the pairs of polarities are closer than they may seem at first. There is, in fact, an *essential* connection underlying sin and madness. Out of the vast region of myth, it is the image of Narcissus that links the two modes of self-understanding: the traditional model of man as sinner, the self "curved in upon itself," and the emergent model of man's madness, the hell of the isolated individual consciousness, which reflects the complexity of man's relationship to man and his fundamental relationship to existence.

But it is not the *half* image of Narcissus, the familiar part to which we are accustomed, that portrays our state. Rather, it is the *whole* myth that reflects our dilemma. The original enigma of the myth has been forgotten. Only if it is restored, will it be possible to focus on a region of dimly understood human experience that reveals us to ourselves, although the portrait may be unflattering. In most versions of the myth, the element that is isolated is that of "self-love." The rest of the story, the result of that "love," is forgotten. Ernest Becker wrote (as Erich Fromm had before him) that the idea of narcissism was "one of Freud's great and lasting contributions. Freud discovered that each of us repeats the tragedy of the mythical Greek, Narcissus: we are hopelessly absorbed with ourselves."[12] Remarkably, the recognition of the implications of the myth stop right there—"we are hopelessly absorbed with ourselves"—and the tale is not carried to its tragic end. After all, Narcissus died of that self-absorption! Strangely, despite verbal acknowledgments, there has been a general denial of that death. Despite the wide use of Greek myth in the symbolism of psychology, curiously little has been done with the myth of Narcissus to illuminate our self-understanding. Even then only part of the myth has been taken into consideration. This is so although "narcissism" is used as a technical term in modern psychology, and despite Freud's assertion that narcissism is the *primary* characteristic of man. Freud himself retreated before the problem that the myth presented, referring to it as the "stone wall of narcissism."[13] What is there, implicit in the myth perhaps—or in our capability to understand it—that has left it so long virtually ignored and unexplored?

The Myth of Narcissus

We all think that we know the myth, but do we really? Let us "play the music backward" to the beginning of the score, to see whether we can "break the enchantment" of the gaze within the mirror. The myth itself—*reconsidered*—[14] will specify our understanding of sin and madness. There are several versions, but lurking behind them all is a terrible split in the soul of Narcissus. Behind the simple tale lies tragedy.[15]

According to the familiar version of Ovid,[16] Narcissus was the son of the nymph Leiriope, who had been ravished by the river-god Cephissus, when he encircled her with the windings of his streams. When Leiriope consulted Tiresias, the seer, about the future of her child he told her, "Narcissus will live to be a ripe old age, provided that he never knows himself."[17]

Narcissus was a boy so compellingly beautiful that many "youths and maidens" fell in love with him. But his stubborn and cold pride, his "hard heart," left him untouched; he rejected them all. Among those he rejected was the nymph Echo, who followed him through the forest seeking his love. But Narcissus shook her off roughly, crying out that he would sooner die than give her power over him. Echo pined away in grief, leaving only her voice. When he spurned Echo, he lived only with "the mind's internal Echo."[18] Narcissus rejected the other nymphs who pursued him just as cruelly. In fact, he actively turned away all suitors. One of them prayed that Narcissus might love and be rejected and not gain the thing he loved. The prayer was heard by Nemesis, who led Narcissus to a pool of water to drink.

It was in the pool that Narcissus saw and fell in love with his own reflection, "unwittingly" it is said, for the image in the water seemed to him to be that of another. Narcissus tried to embrace the loved object, but it fled at his touch and returned again to fascinate him. The image apparently welcomed him. When he approached it, it approached him; when he stretched out his arms to it, it stretched out its arms to him. It seemed to want to be embraced *(cupet ipse teneri)*,[19] yet it fled when touched. In contradictory gestures, it both welcomed and rejected Narcissus. Narcissus could not tear himself away, so preoccupied was he with his own image. At last Narcissus sorrowfully asked the image why it shunned and rejected him. And, as his tears fell in sorrow, they disturbed the image. "And as he saw it vanish, he called after: 'Where are you going? Stay: do not desert me.' "[20] Grieving over the separation, Narcissus entreated the image to remain so that he could gaze on it even though he could not touch it. Narcissus understood his tragedy to be a strange one: "I know the truth at last. . . . I burn with love of my own self."[21] There could be no union with his love —for there was no *other*. The passion with which he burned was self-consuming. He slowly pined away. He loved himself to death. Even Echo, although still angry with him, pitied him as he faded away, until at last "death closed his eyes." But death provided no release. Even in Hades he gazed on his image in the "Stygian pool."

Finally, out of pity for his excruciating suffering, the gods transformed his body into a flower, the narcissus. It is interesting to note its curious properties: the flower is used as a balm, but is apt to give headaches; it was worn when the Erinyes were being placated, indicating the medicinal properties of narcissus oil (the narcotic properties of the flower); but it is more than a narcotic, it is, according to numerous references, poisonous.[22]

Sir James G. Frazer[23] believes that the Ovid version is probably closest to the original, although there are several other versions of the myth, all with variants of the central theme. In an early version by Photius,[24] Narcissus sent his insistent but rejected suitor, Ameinias, a sword with which Ameinias killed himself after praying for vengeance against Narcissus. In all the versions, vengeance occurs when Narcissus becomes his own lover and, unable to endure the grief that is destroying him, commits suicide. Another version, by Pausanias,[25] tells of Narcissus' love for his twin sister and of his grief over her death. Inconsolable, Narcissus would go to the pool pretending to find her reflection there and so relieve his suffering. It has been suggested that Narcissus drowned himself in order to be united with his father, the river-god. It has been said, also, that his death in water symbolizes union with the mother.

In each version the same pattern emerges: Narcissus suffers not merely the despair of the sickness *unto* death—of which one *may* be cured—he actually dies: he "loves" himself to death. According to Grace Stuart:

This at least the legend makes clear. Narcissus' self-loving was, whether actively (the suicide version) or passively (the pining away version), self-destructive. Narcissus actually died of his disease and (in one version) by an act of successful aggression against himself. He was, at one and the same time, a-social, anti-social, and anti-self. . . . Narcissus is . . . a withdrawn person . . . the youth had a surname —"The Taciturn." . . . He withdraws his body to a lonely place and his feelings to the loneliness of his own heart. When, however, the withdrawal has been made, when, at length alone with himself, most literally face to face, Narcissus finds in himself no satisfaction, then he is committed to the gravest of all sufferings. He is the never-to-be-loved lover and from that knowledge he must make the ultimate withdrawal into death.[26]

From that knowledge, as Tiresias warned, he dies.

Echoes of Narcissus

We find the image of Narcissus reflected in the imagination of many writers. Indeed, there are too many for us to do more than suggest their variety. In the fragments of *The Romaunt of the Rose* translated by Chaucer, we find the "proud hearted Narcissus that was in love so dangerous," glancing into "the mirour perilous."[27] Herman Melville wrote that "still deeper the meaning of that story of Narcissus, . . . that same image we ourselves see in all rivers and oceans. It is the image of the ungraspable phantom of life; and this is the key to it all."[28]

"Peer Gynt's Troll philosophy is the inarticulate, the unwitting, philosophy of the narcissist. 'To thyself, be enough is the final antithesis of the capacity to love someone other than oneself.' "[29] In *Le Traité du Narcisse*, André Gide describes the "flaw of man, his sole sin," as his preference for himself, that is, narcissism. "Narcissus was man himself, gazing into the river of time. If he would turn back from the river, he might see other things to love, but he does not turn."[30]

Thus what we see in the image of Narcissus is ourselves. The myth is a profound and penetrating comment on the human dilemma, on our fundamental relationship to the structures of existence, to ourselves, and to others. Narcissus, as a metaphor for the human condition—for our sin, our madness—takes us to that deeper level, that originating point, at which the self divides and at which its intentions diverge, on the one hand grasping love and life, while on the other hand, in that very gesture, embracing death. Narcissism is that sin and that madness by which we unwittingly descend into that nonbeing in which we "love" ourselves to death.

The inherent dialectic is the same in all versions of the myth. Narcissus presents us with a grim portrait of ourselves, implying the highest degree of detachment, inaccessibility, and a self-sufficiency that does not and cannot suffice to sustain us. "What I want is with me, my riches make me poor" *(Quod cupio mecum est; inopem me copia fecit).*[31] The picture reflects the self-encapsulation and anguish that is the consequence of the inability to love and to be loved. It is a portrait, ultimately, of frustration and rejection. Although Narcissus pleads with the image not to reject him, it does. Therefore the myth provides the further suggestion of *self*-rejection, an inability to be one with himself, resulting in a "divided self." The portrait is completed in his abandonment by the "other," with implications of a sense of worthlessness and of rage turned inward. In loving himself to *death,* we find also an "internal saboteur." His was the plight of separation, of estrangement from his loved object, which was no *other* than himself, a mere reflection. Deflected by that reflection from what he considered to be the "true good"—Narcissus "goes astray," to use Pascal's phrase. He goes so far astray, in fact, as to give up his life. "Self-love" was his death. As a consequence of the loss of the "true good everything can appear equally good to him, even his own destruction," as Pascal said. The final image of Narcissus embracing himself in the water makes it dreadfully clear that the final outcome of this ambivalent gesture toward life is death, nonbeing.

Narcissus' despair, which led to his undoing, is man's despair. It is the plight of detachment, estrangement, and lovelessness. It is the theism that has no god *other* than itself. It is self-worship. Narcissus knew too much—the dreadful knowledge that Tiresias warned would be fatal was the knowledge that he was the "never-to-be-loved." He knew that he could neither love nor be loved by an *other*. It was that which filled him with dread. It was that terror which he could not face and which led to his own death.

That Narcissus was "strangely his own lover" suggests a radical disruption in his fundamental relationship to existence. His relation was to none *other* than himself. This is the pathological landscape of the soul revealed by Narcissus. The myth, so understood, is what we have traditionally known as sin and more recently defined as madness. Narcissus, as the paradigm of our relationship to existence, is the metaphor for our "madness," our "sin." Man is a "sick animal," as Pascal said. Being "thrown" into the world *(Geworfenheit)* describes his situation according to the twentieth-century German philosopher Martin Heidegger. Abandoned and living "in exile," alone in the "silence of the infinite spaces," unloved and unable to love, man is "ontologically insecure," insecure about his very being, as Laing has said. In dread—"shut up"—as the nineteenth-century Danish theologian Søren Kierkegaard has said. Man defends himself against the "terror that comes of hope for love and love's defeat"[32] by insulating himself against this condition and against recognizing it. In dread of rejection, in terror of abandonment, Narcissus/man descends into nonbeing. Kierkegaard calls it sin; to Laing it is known as madness.

Narcissus reveals the terror behind the mirror. This is the fate worse than death against which we have anesthetized ourselves, which makes us all victims of amnesia. It is for this fate that we have the narcotic: "eyes that won't see" and "ears that won't hear" and "hearts that are hardened" (Isa. 44:18; Jer. 5:21). Narcissus carries the implications of sin and madness to a deeper level revealing that the consequence of lovelessness and estrangement is an unbearable sense of worthlessness and rejection that is dread-ful. Self-love is the *mask* for that condition. Self-destruction is preferable to the realization of the condition.

It is this predicament—this strategy for survival in the face of the dread of lovelessness, abandonment, rejection, and separation—which may, as with Narcissus, lead us unwittingly to destruction. It is that which divides our consciousness, as well as our intentions, so that we may believe ourselves to be seeking love, when actually it is death that we are embracing. Pride is "death-dealing." Nemesis follows Hubris. Our Nemesis, the vengeance worked on us for our self-idolatry, is our unacknowledged death-embracing intention. That is the internal saboteur that we have projected into history and into culture and onto the environment. It may be that, in ignorance of this, "a civilization of much high achievement is on the verge of making shipwreck."[33] We are warned elsewhere that

we are witless against pride, and it is time that our wits should be gathered together, before it is too late. We have seen pride ride like a winter wind . . . bringing in its train the evil Nemesis; and though the theologians thundered against it, and the tragic poets saw the vision of the darkness ahead, no one could ever banish it entirely from men's hearts. . . . We live in a world where the flame may consume us all. Pride . . . haunts us and may haunt us forever, though we are beginning to learn the nature of the penalty which must be paid— the evidence lies all around us in a world in ruins.[34]

Centuries of wisdom, both of the East and of the West, have taught that in Narcissus' pride—egotheism—lies man's greatest danger. Again and again, we have been warned against this pathology, and persistently shown man's relatedness to an other than self. But what has man learned of these often-repeated lessons? The responses of East and West to the universal human condition of "encapsulation as the general experience of humanity"[35] have been quite different. In the pages that follow we shall hear the ancient wisdom spoken in many voices. We shall also concern ourselves with the evolution of man's madness, with the way in which the pathology of self-encapsulation and estrangement has come about. Finally, in order better to understand the fatality of narcissism, we will examine a modern secular discipline, based on the myth of Narcissus. Psychoanalysis is an evocation of the ancient wisdom in a contemporary idiom.

2
Sin:
The Flight from the Self

At the center of the sickness of the psyche is a sickness of the Spirit. Contemporary psychoanalysis will have to reckon with this Kierkegaardian point of view.

William Barrett[1]

Our nature is so curved in upon itself at its deepest levels that . . . it does not even know that, in this wicked, twisted, crooked way, it seeks everything, including God, only for itself.

Martin Luther[2]

SIN AS A WAY of understanding the disordered human spirit traditionally has focused on pride, or "self-love." It has long been known that the sin of pride is self-destructive, since we are unable to truly love ourselves or our neighbor. But *how* that is so has not been understood. Now, from recent studies, some of which we will examine in a later chapter, we are beginning to gain a somewhat clearer idea. We find from our consideration of the whole myth of Narcissus a description, which is confirmed elsewhere, that suggests that the surface manifestation is what we call a narcissistic preoccupation with the self. A closer reading of the myth, however, suggests a radical shift in our traditional self-understanding. An analysis of the myth takes us a level deeper and cuts through the facade of self-love.

The myth indicates, and the thesis of this book affirms, that the phenomenon of pride, of narcissism,[3] is not inordinate, exaggerated self-love but rather is its opposite—self-hatred, self-destruction. Self-encapsulation or self-enclosure, the apparent self-idolatry of the narcissist, is essentially a defensive maneuver in the face of an overwhelming sense of worthlessness. The "terror of hope for love and love's defeat," paradoxically, ends in an existential death. It is precisely because Narcissus is loveless that he must, as a defense, wrap himself in "self-love." This meaning of the term "narcissism" brings it closer to the core of the myth from which the term is derived. It is also consonant with contemporary clinical data, with the traditional Biblical understanding of man, and with the Eastern understanding of the human predicament. This is what we have known as sin—but with a paradoxical twist or difference.

In an extraordinary way, Søren Kierkegaard's understanding of sin, which stems from the Biblical tradition, confirms this interpretation. It constitutes an analysis of the genesis of narcissism. We could consider the views of Augustine, Blaise Pascal, Thomas Aquinas, or Martin Luther in that same tradition. But Kierkegaard's analysis is the most detailed and his inquiry, especially in relation to anxiety, is the deepest. His analysis of sin elicits a view of man that *assumes* an interpretation, an understanding of pride that is in direct opposition to the usual view as inordinate self-love, for Kierkegaard defines sin in terms of self-destruction. This radical shift from the traditional understanding of pride is often explicitly stated in his analysis of man as "sinner." In a psychologically acute analysis of the self, Kierkegaard[4] unmasks pride to discover that it hides another condition, a fate *worse* than death—the "sickness unto death"[5] (John 11:4) from which one cannot die. Foreshadowing recent research on narcissism, Kierkegaard describes sin as the flight *from*—not love *of*—the self when it falls into a state of dread. Dread precedes and gives rise to sin, he tells us. In this state, in dread over what it may become and threatened with what may become of it, the self shuts itself up in apparent self-love. But this self-enclosure suffocates the self. In dread of abandonment and lovelessness, in dread of being "a nothing" before God, despairing of grace, of being forgiven by God, the sickness unto death results. From this sickness of the self one can be "saved" and restored to health only by God's love.

In a contemporary model of man articulated in the language of phenomenological psychology, Laing also confirms this in-

terpretation, and clarifies and specifies it further. Laing uses
the term "madness" and interprets it as a strategy for survival
in the face of "ontological insecurity," over his very being.
Laing's view of madness carries forward the *meaning* of sin as
we find it in Kierkegaard. Laing interprets madness as the false
self, as self-destruction, but self-destruction as a strategy for
survival in the face of the terror of lovelessness. Here Laing
further specifies the dynamics that are only implicit in Kierkegaard's account. In Laing's view the self has been rejected
in its original nexus and is therefore engaged in a defensive
maneuver, a self-preoccupation as a strategy for survival which,
however, fails. The only hope for the self's cure is by way of
the love of the physician through what remains of the freedom
of the self. In the works of both Kierkegaard and Laing, sin and
madness emerge as ways of understanding pride. Both are
linked *by the image of Narcissus* at their core. We find the
figure of Narcissus—"the self curved in upon itself"[6]—in the
emerging metaphor of madness—the hell of the isolated individual consciousness. Religion and psychology meet in Kierkegaard's brilliant and detailed analysis of the sickness of the
human spirit and in the work of Laing whose correlative diagnosis is of the sickness of the psyche. By engaging in a dialogue
between the model of man as sinner that is rooted in the
Biblical tradition and the contemporary view of madness as the
"divided self," we may be able to look at sin and madness more
clearly in the light of the myth of Narcissus reconsidered.

"The Knot of Our Condition"

We must start by recognizing the paradoxical predicament
that man is a being who must *become* who he is. He must
emerge from a lack of self-awareness into individuality and
self-consciousness. He must discover *that* he is, he must
emerge into a sense of self. His development is not instinctive,
it does not follow the maturational process of nature bound by
necessity. Rather, it is a process that takes place in freedom and
therefore requires decision. Man is a being who is thus a prob-

lem to himself. Implicit in this is the assumption that man has the capacity to evade being himself, to be *self*-destructive, to become, in Bruno Bettleheim's telling phrase, an "empty fortress."[7] This capacity of the self (to become who one is) and its defeat is the locus of the problem and the ground of sin and madness.

We avoid becoming; we use our freedom not to choose ourselves. The "knot of our condition takes its twists and turns in this abyss,"[8] Pascal wrote. Laing echoed this with an implicit emphasis on the bound unconscious will. The problem, although not new, is exacerbated in the modern world. This is considered so central to the human condition that Martin Buber defined man as the "mode of being which evades becoming."[9]

It is this very flight from the self which Kierkegaard and Laing address. The central theme in the writings of both is that man's strategy for survival is to evade becoming himself. Their writings are directed toward disclosing the ways in which the self is lost and to revealing the dynamics of the process of self-destruction—a diagnosis of the human predicament seen by both as sin and as madness.[10]

If man's mode of being is to evade becoming—to seek death and destruction as much as life—one must ask why this is so. This descent into nonbeing, the evasion of becoming, the flight from the self, is understood by Kierkegaard to be sin. This condition starts in the very beginning with Adam, as well as in the infancy of each of us. For the myth of Adam is the story of everyman—each of us is Adam.[11] Every subsequent individual has, does, and shall begin the same way. For every subsequent individual there has been the instant of the "fall." Sin is "original" with each of us. First, let us be clear about this: sin is not a particular misdeed but the predicament man is in. It is not simply neurosis (as has been suggested by some), nor a neurotic maladjustment. Instead, it is a radical disruption of the self, which goes down to our very roots. It is man's life cut off from its Source, its original matrix, and therefore, spiritually "sick unto death." This applies to each of us. As Augustine said, *non posse non peccare* ("It is not possible not to sin"). Kierkegaard tells us that in his infancy man is in a state of "dreaming innocence" in "immediate unity" with his Source and his environment. In this primal state man is ignorant. He lacks self-awareness, a sense of individuality, and freedom with its attendant responsibility. That is, he lacks knowledge of good and evil. The "fall" out of innocence into consciousness—the beginning of self-awareness and individuality, the possibility of one's self as separate being with the potential for freedom and individuality and therefore also of responsibility—is occasioned by a prohibiting, frustrating word.

In the myth, the command prohibiting Adam to eat of the tree of knowledge indicates the possibility of choice: a no, and therefore a possible yes. Adam's choice was between freedom —the responsibility and the necessity to make a decision—and abdication of that responsibility. This word of prohibition signals the separation of the self from its original environment and awakens the possibility of freedom, of self-consciousness, of individuality, which generates dread. Kierkegaard tells us that the "prohibition alarms Adam . . . because the prohibition awakens in him the possibility of freedom, . . . the alarming possibility of *being able.*" The prohibiting word indicates the separation, the freedom required for individuation which is at once fascinating and repelling. Being able—sheer possibility— is alarming. It is dreadful in that it presents an abyss of openness, a nothingness. It awakens one to separatedness and to an unspecified, dizzying freedom into which one *must* move. It suggests, in Kierkegaard's words, the "egotistic infinity of possibility." A further threat accompanies separation from the original environment, for "after the word of prohibition follows the word of judgment: Thou shalt surely die." This evokes a "notion of the terrible," which is also unspecified. The appearance of freedom now indicates that a dreadful possibility may be its consequence. The movement from possibility to reality is filled with dread and premonition of perils because it is not only a movement into the dark unknown but a presentment of evil represented in the myth by the symbol of the serpent. But the myth, Kierkegaard tells us, represents as outward that which is inward. Evil is a possibility into which Adam—man—may willfully move which entails a sickness and ultimately a death of the spirit. "God tempts no man. Every man is tempted by himself." Dread, then, is ambiguous. It is an attitude of the spirit as it would consolidate the self. It is the original conflict from which the original sin arises—the possibility of freedom fascinates and repels simultaneously—one wants and wants *not* to be "able." In this double and contradictory response of dread, this "sympathetic antipathy," the "fall" occurs. Kierkegaard writes: "If we observe children, we find this dread more definitely indicated as a seeking after adventure, a thirst for the prodigious, the mysterious. . . . Even though it alarms him, it captivates him nevertheless, by its sweet feeling of apprehension."

Freedom, even for the infant human, now means defiance of the prohibition with a vague sense of impending doom. And since freedom threatens annihilation, the self falls into a disrelationship. It is no longer in unity but rather in contradiction to its Source, its original environment. In dread, but seeking security in its tenuous relationship with the eternal, the self constricts its freedom and falls out of unity with its Source. It becomes the victim of a sickness of the spirit, in which the factors of the self are thrown out of balance. On the one hand, the self is tempted by the limitless possibilities of infinity to flee from a commitment to be a particular concrete self. Or on the other hand, it is tempted by finitude to reduce the individual to a cipher in the crowd, lost in worldly distractions. It is tempted to evade becoming a self because to choose to be a self is to be threatened by dread.[12] In dread, it falls into despair, the sickness unto death. Kierkegaard describes the process this way:

He whose eye chances to look down into the yawning abyss becomes dizzy. . . . Thus, dread is the dizzyness of freedom which occurs when the spirit would posit the synthesis: and freedom, then, gazes down into its own possibility, grasping at finiteness to sustain itself. In this dizzyness, freedom succumbs. . . . That very instant everything is changed, and when freedom rises again, it sees that it is guilty. Between these two instances lies the leap . . . freedom swoons . . . the fall into sin always occurs in impotence.[13]

Kierkegaard is saying that at the moment of choice, the self uses its fundamental freedom—*to be or not to be*—to choose nonbeing, to retreat into unfreedom, to "fall." The moment of choice occurs at this primal point of transition from nonbeing into being. But, in dread of what it may become or what may become of it, the self is

constantly deferring the movement and [consequently] remain[s] constantly in pain. If a woman in her travail were to get the idea that she might give birth to a monster, or were to ponder within herself what it really was that she would bring forth, her case would be similar to yours. Her effort to check the course of nature would be unavailing but yours is indeed possible, for that to which a man gives birth in a spiritual sense is . . . a [formation] of the will, and that is in a man's own power. What is it then you fear? . . . You are merely to give birth to yourself. . . . It is as though you were caught and ensnared and could never more, either in time or eternity, make your escape, it is as though you lost your own self, as though you cease to be. . . . It is a serious and significant moment . . . when in an eternal and unfailing sense one becomes aware of one's self as the person one is. And yet, one can leave it alone! So here there is an either/or.[14]

Kierkegaard and the Riddle of Narcissus

In his analysis of the fall, Kierkegaard suggests a response to our question: Why is pride ultimately a fatal disorder? The tendency of man to go astray is rooted in the dread of freedom, man's dread of individuation, of separation from immediate unity with his environment and the consequent threat of annihilation.[15] The self defends against this dread by enclosing itself in a protective armor. The self becomes inauthentic, which is ultimately fatal and suffocating. The self has fallen into despair, the sickness unto death, a spiritually fatal illness.

Now, having succumbed, the self *continues* in a dread that deepens the sickness progressively.

In some of us, dread lies hidden and masked—repressed, spiritless—as death in disguise, or lack of consciousness of the self. It is spiritual death because awareness of the self is repressed. In others, dread is manifest as fear of an external happening or fate. This is the response of what Kierkegaard calls the "aesthetic" man. The individual fears fate, but at the same time is attracted to it. If it is an external fate he suffers, he is not responsible, not guilty for his fall into unfreedom. Thus, where there is an awareness of good and evil, in the "ethical" man, dread exists. In dread of evil, the individual is aware of his responsibility for the loss of his self and dreads potential guilt. In dread, he would remove its reality and wish for a return of the self to the state of innocence before freedom was possible and in which he was at one with his environment and therefore neither free nor responsible nor guilty. In remorse, he sorrows over the loss of himself and, in his guilt, considers himself condemned and doomed. Kierkegaard concludes that remorse has "become insane" but it cannot bring the self into being.

Kierkegaard helps us understand the fatality of narcissistic pride in his description of the ultimate form of dread, that of the demoniacal personality (which has nothing to do with a pact with the devil) who exists "in dread of the possibility of the good."[16] Although this is an extreme form of the sickness unto death, it is widespread and "covers a far greater field than is commonly supposed." In fact, "a trace of this is to be found in every man as sure as every man is a sinner." The characteristic of this state of despair is unfreedom. *Originally*, when the individual awakens from the state of innocence and is *faced* with *freedom*, he becomes anxious. He is filled with dread and flees from the possibility for freedom of being an individual. At this deeper level of the disease, having lost freedom and his self, he turns his *back* on it and defends his unfree mode of being. His attitude is: I would keep the "miserable man that I am."

He does not dread what he is but rather dreads the good—that is, the possibility of freedom, the possibility of the release of his "fallen," imprisoned, unfree self.

In dread of the good, the demoniacal personality compulsively avoids contact with it. He retreats deeper and deeper into unfreedom—the self-enclosure by means of which he defends himself. In this state of bondage, he dreads having to leave this mode of being. The attitude toward the possibility of release is dread. The self holds on desperately to the bondage it is in and encloses itself in it as a "safety device." This tenacious self-encapsulation, the refusal to break through into freedom, in fact, to avoid it at all costs, is maintained because the good threatens him with self-destruction. (It is precisely this unauthentic self he must lose to gain his self!) When confronted with the good, the demoniac might beg

for himself . . . that he would not talk to him, would not . . . make him weak. . . . For . . . he . . . has a totality to lose. . . . He would never more be himself. . . . He has given up the good in despair. . . . It well might disturb him. . . . Only in the continuation of sin he is himself. . . . What does this mean? . . . That the state of being in sin is that which, in the depth to which he has sunk, holds him together. . . . It will have nothing to do with the good, will not be weak enough to harken once in a while to another sort of talk. No, it will hear only itself, have to do only with itself, shut itself in with itself, yea, enclose itself. . . . And . . . secure itself against every assault of the good.[17]

As Kierkegaard makes clear, neither Narcissus nor the narcissist is guilty of love of self. Rather, the demoniacal personality in which we all participate to *some* degree is totally self-preoccupied. The self has been negated and this very negation is maintained simply to preserve its being. In the service of that defense, like Narcissus, the self has "eyes that won't see" and "ears that won't hear." "The demoniacal does not shut itself up *with* something, but shuts itself up: . . . unfreedom makes a prisoner precisely of itself. . . . Unfreedom becomes more and more shut up and wants no communication."[18]

Freedom, Kierkegaard tells us, is "expansive," it is "constantly communicating" and making itself known. It is what he calls "transparency." The shut-up, by sharp contrast, is mute and talks only to himself. This "close reserve," or shut-upness, is the effect of the "negating retrenchment of the ego in the individuality." It closes off communication to the point where the victim may "carry the thing so far as to become completely insane, insanity being the pitiful *perpetuum mobile* of monotonous indifference," a discontinuity, a withdrawal from the rest of human life, a break with reality which Kierkegaard calls the "sudden." The demoniacal mode is also depicted as "vacuous" or "tedious." Kierkegaard describes this aspect of the shut-up state as one of ultimate dissatisfaction. It is emptiness, meaninglessness which gives the "impression of being extinct," and a "continuity in nothingness." If this introversion persists, and this melancholy which is "hysteria of the spirit" "is absolutely maintained, . . . then suicide will be the danger nearest to him."[19]

This, then, is Narcissus—a paradigmatic demoniac; Narcissus the Taciturn—a silent, withdrawn person.

He withdraws not only his speech. He withdraws his body to a lonely place and his feelings to the loneliness of his own heart. When, however, the withdrawal has been made, when, at length alone with himself, most literally face to face, Narcissus finds in himself no satisfaction, then he is committed to the gravest of all sufferings. He is the never-to-be-loved lover and from that knowledge he must make the ultimate withdrawal into death.[20]

Kierkegaard confirms this description of the withdrawn personality: the demoniac personality is also the never-to-be-loved. He feels as nothing and suffers a sense of personal unworthiness. The sense of unworthiness, which originally generated the dread of becoming, now creates the possibility of offense —the refusal to believe that the self as sinner can be forgiven. Forgiveness can be accepted only by faith, in the belief that God loves man, "by virtue of the absurd." For it is "absurd"[21] to believe that a man, a sinner, is of sufficient importance to concern God. A man cannot believe that and is offended by the notion.

"Revelation, however, is the first utterance of salvation."[22] The spoken word is precisely the saving thing, that which delivers from the mute abstraction of the shut-up. It breaks the "enchantment of the magic spell." But the demoniac's attitude toward revelation is that he is unwilling to hear it: "Shut-upness may wish for revelation. . . . It may will revelation to a certain degree . . . only to begin all over again with shut-upness. . . . And [it] is cunning enough to transform revelation itself into a mystification." Revelation would be the beginning of the health, of salvation of the self, but shut-upness is in conflict about it. "He has, in fact, two wills, one of them subordinate, impotent, which wills revelation and a stronger will which wills to be shut-up." The more the demoniac is determined to be the self he *wills* to be, the deeper he sinks into the sickness of despair, until he develops a truly demoniac rage. If God himself offered to help him, he would refuse, for "he would rather rage against everything" and keep his torment to justify his rage.

It is (to describe it figuratively) as if an author were to make a slip of the pen, and that this clerical *error* [emphasis supplied] became conscious of being such. . . . It is then as if this clerical error would revolt against the author out of hatred for him or to forbid him to correct it, and were to say, "No, I will not be erased, I will stand as a witness against thee, that thou art a very poor writer."[23]

Kierkegaard's Theory of Therapy

The demoniac will *hear* nothing of what might free him. In fact, he will not believe, in despair of the good, that forgiveness is possible.[24] However, Kierkegaard points out, "there is a method applicable to such a case which, perhaps, is rarely used: it is silence. . . . If an inquisitor has the requisite physical strength and spiritual elasticity to hold out . . . though it were for 16 hours, he will, at last be rewarded by the admission (the secret of the demoniac) breaking out involuntarily. . . . The only power which can compel shut-upness to speak is either a higher demon . . . or the good, which is absolutely silent."[25] Kierkegaard's theory of therapy anticipates modern theories in as startling a fashion as does his diagnosis of the condition. It will be sketched in roughly here, so that we may refer back to it when we discuss the techniques for scaling the "stone wall of narcissism" that have been developed in recent years.

As we have seen, dread is originally the obstacle to the self's venture to become itself. The continuation of that dread resists the cure or the restoration of the self. As dread was the barrier to the original act of choice of the self, dread also continues to obscure consciousness and corrupt the will, moving the individual defiantly in contradiction to its true self. Dread resists reversing this negation, but it is also the means of healing. It remains in the individual all through the therapeutic process and intensifies as the self gets closer to restoration.

Kierkegaard says that, for a "healing from the very bottom," it is necessary to be "rightly in dread." What does that mean? Dread lies always at the juncture of possibility and reality. It indicates, in fact, the "possibility of freedom."[26] Dread teaches the individual. It is educative because it can consume all trivial, finite concerns that are peripheral to being a self and reveals their deceptiveness. One can always, Kierkegaard says, "talk them around," use them as diversions, escapes, and so prevent one's self from being educated to be a self. Dread frees one to "learn absolutely," that is, to become who one is. In order to do that, one must be "honest toward possibility" and faithfully stay with dread. The seemingly dreadful things of everyday life diminish in comparison with those of the possibility of being one's self. Therefore, "only the man who has gone through the dread of possibility is educated to have no dread." The pupil of possibility, the individual who will learn in spite of, know because of, dread "receives infinity"—that is, his unique self. He who betrays possibility is trapped and lost in the finite.

It is education by dread that makes the restoration of the self, or what Kierkegaard calls "repetition," possible, for the self is a possibility that has become lost in dread. The possibility that the ideal image of the self can become actual must be brought into existence by an existential remembering, a "putting together," repeated forward in life. To "know thyself"— to recall a past existence—was the recommendation of Socrates. To "choose thyself" is Kierkegaard's prescription, to reduplicate existentially what originally existed only as a possibility. To imply that it is possible to recover one's self by "recollection" is to assume that to understand about the self is sufficient. In fact, what is necessary is the willingness to be—the will to choose—one's self.

But what therapeutic method is appropriate for bringing a self into existence? The problem lies—as Kierkegaard emphasizes in his distinction between objective or "disinterested" truth (e.g., of mathematics or science) and existential or "concerned" truth (the relation of the thinker to his thought)—in its appropriation to his existence. The test of this kind of truth is not logical but psychological. Existential truth is not the rational solution of a conceptual problem, but the personal resolution of an existential predicament.

Kierkegaard understood that only negative teaching is possible. Men are polemic against the truth, intentionally fleeing it. He used indirect communication in his writings, rather than intellectual understanding, in order to provoke a choice of the self—"repetition." Communication *about* the individual would not be appropriate to the process of self-discovery, which Kierkegaard hoped to evoke. For this purpose, he employed a kind of communication that would "cut and cauterize for healing," a language appropriate to becoming, for the self is what it is to become. Kierkegaard's purpose was to disturb and provoke the reader into being himself, since he is fleeing, negating, himself. This contradiction within the self requires a form of communication in which this can be reflected. Therefore, he finds that an "elusive form of communication is the only adequate one."[27] It is not direct, it is deceptive; that is, "it begins by accepting the other man's illusion as good money."[28] It starts where the individual is in his life and goes along with the self and its negative movement, accepting and mirroring its illusions and pretensions, reflecting the understanding that exists.[29] The purpose is to lead the individual to a *choice* between the negative and the positive ways—to keep the "wound of the negative open, which . . . is sometimes the condition for a cure,"[30] since the self is ambivalent in its dread and wants not to be a self. Hence, although this indirect way of luring the individual out of his illusions is ultimately insufficient, Kierkegaard's indirect method was a technique to "trick" the self into recognizing the negative direction in which it is moving, to expose his unauthentic existence, and to nudge him to move through life's stages on the way to becoming a self.

The goal of Kierkegaard's therapeutic is to jolt the individual from one stage of life to the next—but with his concurrence —since the self exists in freedom. As he puts it, "if anyone is to profit by this sort of communication [indirect], he must himself undo the knot for himself."[31] In order for repetition to take place, the self must shed the layers of its hiddenness and become transparent. In so doing, it will move from the deepest layers of hiddenness and unselfconsciousness through the various levels of existence—the aesthetic, the ethical, and the religious—on the way to becoming a self.

On the aesthetic level, which is characterized by "immediacy," the individual is involved in seeking pleasure. He is involved in finite goals made into absolute ends. This results in boredom. The self lives at its own expense until it has become bankrupt or has lost itself.

When the self becomes aware of this bankruptcy, which is Kierkegaard's purpose, the aesthetic level is no longer an existential possibility. The irony of its existential situation dialectically precipitates the self into the ethical state. In order for this to occur, the "immediate" man must make the *initial* movement of resignation, relinquishing finite goals as a prerequisite for the journey through the stages to selfhood. A commitment to selfhood requires a dying away to immediacy, that is, a shedding of his old self. This essentially means suffering, that is, an acceptance of the Absolute to define the purpose of one's life, to become "helpless in self surrender." Suffering lies in the "expression, existentially, of the principle that the individual can do absolutely nothing of himself, but is as nothing before God. . . . This consciousness of impotence, he requires constantly to have before him.[32] This means that the self is in limbo, in despair. He is no longer determined by worldly finite goals, but neither is he able to reach his ultimate goal.

Once he has made the movement of resignation and thereby has willed to choose himself, he discovers he is helpless—impotent to become himself, for the movement of faith is not possible from within himself. It must be granted to him. One needs God. Another way to understand this is as the relation between the "first self" and the "deeper self," as Kierkegaard puts it. Properly to see the self is to see it in relation to God as the Other. To regard the self in relation to God is what is dreadful, for "instead of being master of his fate, he becomes a needy petitioner; instead of being able to do everything, he can do nothing at all."[33] When, however, a "man turns about so as to confront himself . . . it is as if he blocked the way for that first self. . . . He calls the first self away from external things. . . . The deeper self . . . proceeds to picture the outer world . . . and its mutability in such terms that it no longer seems desirable to the first self." Then the crucial moment of decision is at hand: *"Either* the first self must contrive to slay the deeper self, to plunge it into oblivion, when all is lost; *or* it must admit that the deeper self is right." For sin has been precisely the rejection of this self.

When the first self and the deeper self are reconciled, new dangers must be met. For "a more profound self knowledge teaches one precisely that one needs God." However, we are ahead of ourselves, for the self has not yet reached that level. Precipitated onto the ethical level, the self is concerned with duty and responsibility, but discovers in his finite attempt to realize infinite ethical goals he is guilty, that is, conscious of not being himself. This is the *decisive* expression of the pathos of existence. In consciousness of disrelationship—"wrongness"—the self accepts the essential guilt of the finite individual in relation to an infinite goal. An individual cannot go beyond this level on his own. Faith comes from beyond the individual's ability to venture. It is the offer of forgiveness from God *to* the self. As we have seen, the offer cannot be believed.

The goal of Kierkegaard's therapeutic is to provoke the individual to "leap" from one stage of life to the next in order to become the self one is in relation to God as Other—through self-transcendence. In order for "repetition" of the original potential self to come about, the self must shed successive layers of its hiddenness—to become "transparent." As Kierkegaard puts it, leaps signify a crisis and a negation of a previous state. At this point of crisis, a man is bound to be in the dark about himself. He will be in a state of dread, which forebodes a disruption in his existence, for it indicates the untenable position in which he finds himself and the dreadful decision to be made. This is the junction of possibility and reality, at which point the self *either* remains faithful to the state of dread *or* falls.

There is no rational, logical, continuous transition from one mode of being to another. The movement from potentiality to actuality of the self takes place in a discontinuous manner. The becoming of the self involves, rather, a personal resolution of the existential predicament in which one is, which comes about in different ways, at different levels of existence, but *always* with the individual's concurrence, because the self exists in freedom.

The individual is powerless to go farther on his own. Although dread can indicate the way, what is finally necessary— faith—can come only from beyond the individual's capacity to venture alone. In his impotence to become himself, his being "as nothing before God," he is made aware of being a "sinner." He is made aware that he is dependent on, but cut off from, his Source. This is the predicament man is in—and from which he cannot extricate himself. This truth man cannot know of his own accord, since he is in the very condition that obscures it. The truth must be revealed to him from without. The appropriate method of communication of the truth at this point is no longer the indirect method of negation of the self-dispelling illusion—but rather of bearing witness to the truth. The revelation is of God's love and offer of forgiveness. This is the gospel —the Communication from a Witness to the truth who is also the Object of Faith. It is the individual's relation to the Object of Faith that effects an alteration of the self: it recognizes itself as lost—as separated from its Source—and also identifies with the ideal Image that it would become.

In this reciprocal relationship between God and man, what is God's claim on man and with what does man respond? It is the self that recognizes that instead of being master of his fate he is actually dependent upon and related to an Other. In this faithful relationship, the defensive, encapsulated, constructed self can surrender to its true self. Although the struggle is painful, the "deeper self . . . knows that this sickness is not unto death but unto life." In sum, Kierkegaard's therapeutic by "indirect communication" mirrors the self in its flight from itself to bring it ultimately to a recognition of what one is not, while his "direct communication" points to the Revelation of what the self can be and offers "forgiveness." For Kierkegaard the self is educated by dread to faith, to be itself, or is lost in "self-slaughter."

Kierkegaard makes clear the fatality of pride, the fate worse than death from which Narcissus suffered. He sees it as a "tragic paradox" that the more the self is defended by the refusal to be itself, by self-enclosure, the more it is destroyed. In its attempt to save itself it becomes lost. In this dialectic the self chooses not life, but death. Kierkegaard's therapy is meant to undo pride and to recall the self to the faith that God forgives one and that God is love. His therapeutic would turn self-destruction into proper self-concern, into self-realization in the context of a relation with the Other. It would turn the self from a sense of unworth and guilt, being "as nothing before God," from complete despair and helplessness, and via forgiveness from self-negation into self-acceptance and relationship with the Other. Only faith discovers that dread does not threaten annihilation but the "fear of the Lord" is the beginning of wisdom—that it is the choice of life, not death. Faith reverses the rejection of grace and means the willingness to lose one's self in order to gain one's self. It is openness to "hearing the words of the Lord," to the incursion of grace.

This is also Laing's view. He agrees with Kierkegaard that defensive self-enclosure is a strategy for survival that fails. Reversal of flight from the self and breaking through shut-upness is required for cure. However, as we shall see in the following chapter, his views are set in the context of the modern idiom of phenomenological depth psychology—and sin is understood as madness.

3
Madness:
The Divided Self

> One who makes terror rather than love the center of his work, knowing all the while, of course, that there can be no terror without the hope for love and love's defeat.
>
> *Leslie Fiedler*[1]

> Love is precluded and dread takes its place.
>
> *R. D. Laing*[2]

> The self in such a schizoid organization . . . enters the condition called by Kierkegaard "shutupness."
>
> *R. D. Laing*[3]

THE METAPHOR of madness that has been emerging in recent years reflects the condition that Kierkegaard understood as sin. By this term he meant the shut-upness, encapsulation, falsification, and loss of the self. Kierkegaard understood the condition to be a withdrawal of the self when confronted with dread in the face of freedom, which simultaneously beckons and threatens. The response of dread results in a conflict that paralyzes the self and is the occasion for its fall. Ronald D. Laing, in a view of man that takes issue with the medical model of madness as disease, understands this unresolvable conflict to be the ground from which madness arises. For him, madness is the estrangement of the self, the divided self. But Laing goes a level deeper and specifies the withdrawal as a defensive strategy for survival in an untenable situation. He also understands the falsification of the self to be a withdrawal in the face of dread, an ontological insecurity of a self incapable of autonomy. Detachment and isolation are regarded as the only possible alternatives to dependence on the other who is necessary for one's being, yet also a threat. What was *implicit* in Kierkegaard's tale of Adam and the Fall is *explicit* in Laing's writings. "The Dreadful" has already happened, Laing writes. The self has been rejected, abandoned, threatened with a word of prohibition, and a subsequent word of punishment. For Laing, this happened to the self in the family, its original nexus; for Kierkegaard, it was in the Garden of Eden—*man*'s original nexus. Each sin is original sin.

Divided Self: Strategy for Survival

Therefore, Laing says, we live in "divided and distinguished worlds."[4] Instead of being whole, and having the requisite "twofold vision" that William Blake prescribed, we are divided: Experience is divorced from behavior. Faith—the experience of Presence—is separated from belief, a conviction in respect to the existence of God. Sanity is adapting to external reality, while madness is entering into an estranged, internal reality. Laing suggests that we remember Kierkegaard's "objective madness,"[5] since Kierkegaard also saw the absence of inwardness as madness and stated that his purpose was to remind us what it means to exist as human beings. The deletion of "subjectivity"—the radical estrangement from the inner world (inwardness)—is sin, as it is madness. Kierkegaard spoke of a person in such a condition as a "madman" and as an "artificial product." Laing identifies such a person as a false self. As Kierkegaard says, "he suffers from . . . a derangement of feeling, the derangement consisting in his not having any."[6]

Kierkegaard and Laing see the problem as manifested in "objectivity." Objectivity is the form of madness, in which, as Kierkegaard sees it, thought is divorced from existence, logic from life. As Laing sees it, inner is estranged from outer, experience alienated from behavior, so that the very existence of inner reality is questioned. One who moves into that inner reality then appears mad. Inwardness has become nonexistent, so the madness of objectivity becomes rampant.

Then, we are *all* divided selves. This is a schizophrenic age.

We are split off from our true selves. What Laing initially said only of the "labeled schizophrenic," he ultimately applied to every man, since all of us are "only two or three degrees Fahrenheit from experiences of this order."[7] We are not "hearing words of the Lord." The discrepancy between our experience and our behavior is the underlying theme of all of Laing's work and it widens so that it takes on universal proportions.

In Laing's schema, the polarity between sanity and madness (true self/false self) acquires the significance of the traditional polarity between faith and sin, although they are not exact equivalents. Each of us is Adam and each fallen. The "dreadful" has already happened. For Laing as for Kierkegaard, each of us in some degree becomes Narcissus. As Freud said, each of us repeats the tragedy of the mythical Greek, Narcissus.

How does Laing describe the human situation? How can I say that his model of madness now carries the weight of what Kierkegaard describes as sin—understood in the light of the myth? How does Laing's description confirm the significance of the myth of Narcissus? What is the dreadful that has happened?

Laing's description of ontological insecurity sounds for all the world like Kierkegaard's dread, and the mythological portrayal of the fate of Narcissus. Laing says that he is concerned with the consequences of an existential position of "primary ontological insecurity" and the attempts to deal with that position. It is a position in which "human nature is deeply implicated,"[8] and which Laing ultimately sees as a universal human condition. Ontological insecurity means that the individual fears the loss of his very being. He has no sense of his own reality, no sense of his validity and worth, to counterbalance his despair. Rather, he feels more dead than alive. He flounders in the void, and is preoccupied with preventing himself from falling into the abyss of nonbeing, into total nothingness. Above all, the ontologically insecure individual fears the dissolution of his self. Everyday life presents him with continual, deadly threats of descending into nonbeing. His primary concern is with preserving his self. It is, in fact, his fundamental project.[9]

This project is a project manqué, for it is doomed to fail by the very nature of the human mode of being. Laing says, "Our alienation goes to the roots."[10] Man is open to the threat of moral, spiritual, and physical forms of annihilation; hence, no one escapes it. To this threat Laing adds the ontological insecurity of a divided self. In this the individual encounters nonbeing as a loss of the unity of the self, a loss of relatedness with others, and, in the extreme form, a chaotic nonbeing in which relatedness to self and to others is totally severed.

Laing considers the preliminary anxiety to be basically the threat of annihilation ("Thou shalt surely die").[11] This is, evocative of Kierkegaard's concept of the dread of the dissolution of the self into nonbeing. No matter how it is described, the defensive response is the same: paradoxically it is to attempt to avoid being in order to escape annihilation. The individual "descends into a vortex of non being in order to avoid being, but also *to preserve being from himself*" (emphasis supplied), for if

there is anything the schizoid individual is likely to believe in, it is his own destructiveness. . . . He regards his own love and that of others as being as destructive as hatred. . . . His isolation is not entirely for his own self's sake. It is also out of concern for others. . . . What he may then do is to destroy, "in his mind" the image of anyone or anything he may be in danger of becoming fond of, out of a desire to safeguard that other person or thing, in reality, from being destroyed. . . . In the last resort, he sets about murdering his "self" and this is not as easy as cutting one's throat.[12]

To play dead is a strategy devised to secure the self against feeling overwhelmed and threatened by anxiety in relationships with other people. The self may feel endangered by different forms of anxiety and defends itself as did Narcissus, by self-enclosure. The ontologically insecure person may feel threatened by the possibility of engulfment, by being absorbed by another, in dread that he may lose his identity in relationship. To preserve himself under this pressure, his defense is isolation. Instead of being able to maintain a balance between separateness and relatedness, like Narcissus he must have complete aloneness. "His longing [as with Narcissus] is for complete union. But of this longing he is terrified, because it will be [as it was for Narcissus] the end of his self."[13] Or he may feel the possibility of being crushed. Since he is "empty," the pressure of reality from outside will overwhelm him. He feels subject to "implosion." Contact with reality, then—as with Kierkegaard's demoniac who fears the intrusion of reality behind his barricade—threatens his existence. Still another dread looms in the possibility of "petrification"—the terror of being scared stiff—of becoming a "thing" or an "it." The dread of so losing one's subjectivity tends to make the individual maneuver others into precisely the same position as a way of dealing with the threat. To depersonalize, to deaden the other, or to be oneself eliminates the threat of being deadened by another person.

The Locked Door

A person-to-person relationship is manifestly impossible where there is dread of losing one's self, dread of dissolution, at the very core of one's being. Laing has found that the very danger dreaded functions dialectically as a means of escaping the danger. To feign death becomes the means of remaining alive; to safeguard one's autonomy, one locks it up. And so it was with Narcissus and Kierkegaard's self. In dread of freedom, the self uses its freedom to make a prisoner of itself. Despite the contradictory dread of being drained of its existence by the other, the self cannot *be* by itself. It is felt to be bound up with and dependent on the other for its existence. There is no possibility here of mutual relationship in which the self is both related to and yet separate from the other.

It would be a profound error, Laing believes, to consider

such self-concern and self-preoccupation narcissistic in any proper application of the term.[14] "The self in this condition is unable to fall in love with its own reflection." Precisely! This preoccupation is not, Laing is saying, narcissism in the usual sense. It is, however, narcissism as *we* have been discussing it, an apparent self-love that is self-destructive. It attempts to be a defense against the threats of life and yet it turns out to be a strategy for survival that results in self-destruction. In avoiding dread, by avoiding being one's self, the self "falls" into nonbeing. Laing explains that "to consume one's self by one's own love prevents the possibility of being consumed by another."[15] Inordinate self-preoccupation is a total mode of being-in-the-world based on a profound sense of worthlessness and fear of self-loss.

Referring his reader to Kierkegaard, Laing says that "schizophrenia cannot be understood without understanding despair."[16] The forms of this sickness of despair are determined by the *modus vivendi* that the self works out in its attempt to hold "the center" of its being from falling apart. Paradoxically, this *modus vivendi* is to split the self in two—to become a divided self—embodied and disembodied, behavior divorced from experience, inner from outer, true self from false self. The body is looked upon in this division as the core of a false self that is a disguise to defend the inner or true self in the world. By avoiding participation in the world, it remains "safe." It is a refuge against engulfment, implosion, and petrification. Wanting no communication, as Laing says, the self

enters the condition called by Kierkegaard "shut-upness." . . . The self . . . shut up with itself, regards itself as the "true" self and the personnae as false. . . . The individual is developing a microcosmos within himself; but . . . this autistic, private . . . "world" is not a feasible substitute for the only world there really is, the shared world.[17]

But it is precisely the shared world of relationships that the self cannot abide any more than Narcissus could. It is safe only in its enclosure. Since this project—to so preserve himself—is not possible, it "leads on to persistent despair," or, in Kierkegaard's terms, the "sickness unto death."

In this despair the self becomes "dead," "Spiritless." It cultivates a death in life in defense against the pain of life. Kierkegaard had said that in despair the self "would be rid of himself." Laing agrees that the self's strategy for survival can become an intentional project of self-annihilation because the individual feels guilty over his very existence. He feels rotten and unworthy to "occupy space" or to seem of value to anyone. In dread of being himself, he tries to be nobody. But, then, he feels dead. On the other hand, if he tries to affirm his existence, he feels painfully that this is a pretense because, after all, he is worthless. For him "all love was disguised persecution." He has, Laing says, "two entirely antithetical . . . sources of guilt: One urge[s] him to life, the other urge[s] him to death."[18]

Laing makes a useful distinction between authentic and inauthentic guilt: *inauthentic* guilt drives one toward the goal of being nobody, which in turn drives one into *authentic* guilt at having died. As Laing says, the individual

feels guilty at daring to be and doubly guilty at not being, at being too terrified to be, and attempting to murder himself, if not biologically, then existentially. His guilt is the urgent factor in preventing active participation in life, and in maintaining the "self" in isolation, in pushing it into further withdrawal. Thereupon, guilt becomes attached to this very manoeuver, which was prompted by guilt originally.[19]

Using its freedom to isolate itself from danger, the encapsulated inner self, in effect, negates itself and qualifies that very freedom. In dread, in ontological insecurity, the self descends into nonbeing in an attempt to preserve its being. Relationship to others and the world—which would enliven it, also threatens to slay it. The self is literally "beside itself." The inner or true self, then, is not revealed, but hidden. All that is visible to the world is the body—the false self—"an empty fortress."

The Other

Wholeness, an integral sense of identity, requires the existence of another person by whom one is known. The importance of "the other" in Laing's view is reflected in his understanding that a person's identity can never be completely abstracted from his identity for others.[20] However, the relation to others is ambivalent (Kierkegaard also suggests we be "chary"), for "the others can contribute to his self-fulfillment or they can be a potent factor in his losing himself . . . even to the point of madness."[21] Here, Laing diverges not only from Kierkegaard, whose consideration of the other is minimal in the development of the self, but also from Freud's "monadic" psychology in his description of the self as an intrapsychic drama. Laing emphasizes interpersonal relations: the self in a social nexus and as a mode of being in the world. True self-transcendence means relationship. But in this transcendence *in vacuo* in which the self is volatilized, "love is precluded and dread takes its place. . . . What one might call a *creative relationship* with the other . . . is impossible, and an *interaction* is substituted . . . which has no 'life' in it (*sterile* relationship). There is a quasi it-it interaction instead of I-thou realtionship. This interaction is a dead process."[22] It is this state of shut-upness that Kierkegaard described as the tedious, as deadness, as boredom. Separation is not only the word for sin but also the other name for madness just as death is the other name for Narcissus.

Laing traces this fatality back to the "original nexus" of the self, as Kierkegaard did mythically and poetically for Adam and therefore for all of us. The dreadful, he says, has already happened. What does that mean? Laing understands that the dreadful occurs *between* people. In order to understand a person's existential stance, it is necessary, Laing says, to understand what "original sense of place in the world he was given in the first instance by the 'nexus' of original others."[23] The self can be put into a false position, or an untenable one, by the actions of others. Although the self universally seems to desire a place of first importance, or certainly of significance, in an other's world, it may be that the self is given no place at all. In that case it has no presence for others and feels guilty to occupy any place at all. It has no sense of what it means to exist, to be somebody. As Buber has said, love and hate confirm the existence of an other, but sheer indifference, the inability to make any difference, denies one's right to be a self.

The self that feels guilty to occupy any space in the world withdraws into himself. But he also becomes "self-conscious," which is defined by Laing as "an awareness of one's self, by one's self, and an *awareness of oneself as an object of someone else's observation.* "[24] Such self-awareness, and knowing others are aware of him, assures him that he exists. Consciousness of one's self in time, preoccupation with the self, assures one's continuity. Self-forgetfulness, absorption in anything outside the self, threatens confusion of self and other and hence the loss of the self. Laing tells of a patient who reported that she had forgotten herself at a carnival one evening. She became so absorbed in it that she forgot the time and forgot who and where she was. When suddenly she realized she hadn't been aware of herself, she became dreadfully frightened. She felt she must never forget herself for a minute, or she loses track of who she is.

Self-consciousness, however, also presents a risk: *To be* is *to be seen.* But to be seen is also to be vulnerable to the dangers of being observed by another, when one is unsure of one's being and ambivalent about the other. Dread of being exposed to the "Look," as Jean-Paul Sartre called it, is counteracted by being invisible—opaque, in Kierkegaard's terms—blending into the environment, as Laing quotes a patient as saying, or becoming one of the "crowd," as Kierkegaard suggested we do to avoid being ourselves. In this state of self-consciousness, the self is endangered by the gaze of others and "under the evil eye of his own scrutiny."[25] Being visible and being invisible are both equally impossible because both involve loss of the self. As Kierkegaard understood it, the self cannot *be* and it cannot *not* be, that is, it cannot die. It cannot be transparent and it cannot be opaque. This is an untenable situation. To preserve this self from nonbeing, the strategy is to maneuver into a position of not being oneself.

Laing traces the basic elements of this precariously structured self back to early infancy. In the original nexus, the other is the mother or, more broadly, the "mothering one." The individual whose existence has not been recognized—has not been "seen" as a person in his own right—cannot *be* himself for fear of what he might be in actuality. He becomes compliant. "The nature of the mother as the first 'object' will . . . be reflected—the mirror image of the legend (of Narcissus) comes naturally back—in the nature of the child."[26] Laing says that the fear of losing one's self, of disappearing, "is closely associated with the fear of . . . [the] mother disappearing. It seems that loss of the mother at a certain stage threatens the individual with loss of himself."[27] As Kierkegaard knew, separation from one's Source threatens the self. Laing associates the need to be perceived in order to exist with the child's fear of the disappearance of the mother under whose loving eye it exists, whose presence lends it its being, whose absence threatens its loss. He takes up Freud's suggestion that in fear of the disappearance of the mother the child makes both the mother and himself disappear in an attempt "to master the anxiety of a danger situation by repeating it again and again in play." The child could split himself in two so that one part functioned as self and the other as observer of himself, as "being there"— although it was only a reflection of himself. In "overcoming or attempting to overcome the loss or absence of the real other in whose eyes he lived and moved and had his being, he becomes another person to himself who could look at him from the mirror." Like Narcissus, he withdraws into himself and his mirror image or rather he makes of his mirror image an other.

The "schizoid person seeks . . . [by] way of being a mirror to himself, to turn his self, a quasiduality with an overall unity, into two selves, that is, into an actual duality."[28] What better description could we have of Narcissus who not only withdraws into himself but who seeks, by way of his watery image, to be with it and to be lovingly perceived by an other? Laing points out that perception or the need to be perceived is fundamentally associated with being. It is only in the mother's presence that the child is able to have his being confirmed. Hence, the night-light makes it possible for him to see himself, or when going to sleep the child needs to be seen by another to nullify the terror that is in the darkness.

But beyond this visual sense, there is the universal need of the child to have his existence confirmed by the mother. Laing suggests that for the infant to be seen is only one of many ways in which the needs of the infant are met. His body is fondled and touched to a degree that it will not be again. It may well be that a lack of responsiveness on the mother's part to the being of the infant will have significant consequences. In other words, if the mother does not recognize the child's existence as a person in his own right, then the child cannot be himself. The child couples outward compliance (being "good") with inner isolation. Out of the dread of being itself, the false self arises. The false self assumes the characteristics of the other, in its compliance, but since the other is loved, the self becomes hateful to itself. In this insufficient differentiation between itself and the other of whom it is a reflection the self becomes lost in its attempt to save itself.

What Kierkegaard has put in terms of the self's relationship to its Source, Laing has expressed in relation to the "mothering one." Although it is not wise to blur the distinctions between the relative and the Absolute, we should note that for an infant, the mothering one is certainly the omnipotent other. The threat of annihilation in one's original nexus, as with Adam, leaves one in dread of being and in flight from the self.

The word "narcissism" comes readily back on its cue. The Narcissist is, by one definition, an insufficiently differentiated person, the sequence of events in his making being something like this. Without an early experience of a sufficient love, he has not been, not become a securely independent person—not created a core of himself—and unless he becomes an independent person, he cannot himself, in turn, love. . . . We love out of leisure from self-concern, and we are always self-concerned unless we know that someone other than ourself is prepared to maintain the significance of our being.[29]

Without confirmation by another, at once "the simplest and the most difficult thing," the existence of a person, his right to a place in the world, his right to be, is given no recognition. It is, in fact, denied. He is rendered ontologically insecure. A confirmatory reaction is one in which the other gives a direct response, one that is relevant to the action and the person in the moment.

It is common sense, Laing says, that a person could put himself into a false existential position, to conceal and attempt to annihilate himself, although he might be unaware of so doing. This is what Kierkegaard described as the depth of despair, not willing to be one's self and, as Laing himself points out, at the same time not conscious of being in despair. To put one's self in that position, as Kierkegaard understood it, is sin, a position that is a matter of one's will. For Laing, to be such a false self is madness, although it is a position into which one is put by others, by the lack of confirmation one is given.

The Double Bind

Ontological insecurity may also be engendered by another form of interpersonal interaction. This is a positive form of disconfirmation (in contrast to the failure of responsiveness of the mother, just described). It is related to Kierkegaard's understanding of dread and has come to be known as the "double bind." Others can make a person's position ultimately untenable by attempts to drive him crazy. In general, it can be said that the attempt to drive another crazy functions at an unconscious level. It can be characterized by the kind of interpersonal interaction that "activates areas of the personality in opposition to one another. This promotes confusion in respect to identity of self, other and situation until ultimately the self is mystified and alienated."[30] The confusion it creates masks the true issues and puts the person in a position where he is damned if he does and damned if he doesn't because the victim is caught in a crosscurrent of contradictory injunctions. No matter in which direction he moves, his actions, his being, cannot be confirmed. He comes to feel all "wrong" and "worthless."

This sort of disintegrative conflict which fosters confusion and mystification is characteristic of the genesis of the schizophrenic personality. The "double bind" thesis of Gregory Bateson and his associates,[31] to which Laing subscribes, states that two people are involved—the "victim" and a member of the family. There is repeated experience of contradictory injunctions (reminiscent of the ambivalent gesture of the image of Narcissus, seeming to welcome, yet eluding him). There is a "primary negative injunction" with a threat of punishment. There is also a "secondary injunction conflicting with the first," also enforced with "punishments that threaten survival" but that are communicated nonverbally. "A tertiary negative injunction," which adds to the threat to survival of the individual, involves an injunction not to escape from the doubly bound situation or to recognize it. This double-bind pattern is finally adopted by the "victim" as his way of perceiving the world. Unable to break through, the self is "shut up" in an "untenable position" in which he cannot move without being threatened with annihilation. Finally, through recurrent experience the "victim" automatically sees the world in patterns that duplicate the double-bind situation—any aspect of which can "precipitate panic or rage." Bateson concludes that anyone who is repeatedly subjected to such incompatible demands will find it difficult to remain sane. Laing draws a crucial conclusion from past studies—that if "patients were *disturbed,* their families were often very disturbing."[32] Bateson points out that "we must look not for some specific traumatic experience in the infantile etiology, but rather for characteristic sequential patterns" in response to which the patient's "unconventional communication habits will be . . . appropriate. The hypothesis which we offer is that sequences of this kind in the external experience of the patient are responsible for the inner conflicts of Logical Typing."[33]

The double bind, "a paradigm of an insoluble, can't win situation, specifically destructive of self-identity and not obvious to the protagonists," forces the self to devise a strategy for survival that may mean going mad. In fact, Laing writes, "without exception the experience and behavior that gets labelled schizophrenic is a special strategy that a person invents in order to live in an unlivable situation."[34] What violence we do with "love"! Poetically and mythically Kierkegaard conveys the same sense: "in dread, in relation to the prohibition and the punishment,"[35] alarmed and yet captivated, for dread is a sympathetic antipathy, in the impotence of that "double bind," the self falls. Having received a double communication, the possibility of being able countered by a command of prohibition and a threat of punishment, freedom beckoning yet threatening, the self breaks down. Narcissus' reflection beckoned and retreated, welcomed and abandoned, in ambivalent gestures suggestive of the double bind.

Inevitably, one is first defined by others. Yet one has the choice between selecting that definition of self, which is not necessarily what one believes one's self to be, or breaking away from this identification and creating another identity and seek to persuade others to confirm it. Laing interprets the injunction by Jesus to leave one's parents (Matt. 19:5) to mean that the self must neither allow its life to pivot around a role given it by others nor confirm it negatively by "demonic will."

Unlocking the Door: Therapeutic Strategies

The "way out is via the door," Laing says. But the means of effecting a "cure" are not so simple. Although Laing does not explicitly describe a therapeutic procedure, there are several indications of his general theoretical views. In his initial suggestions, psychotherapy is based on the principle that we live in the polarity relatedness/separateness and that that relatedness remains a possibility for even the most isolated and withdrawn human beings. That possibility is used to break through the individual's extreme separateness, isolation, and self-enclosure. Laing emphasizes that the therapist must understand the patient's existential position, his way of being in the world as a person, rather than impose categories for understanding his behavior. The relationship between therapist and patient, rather than the classical clinical detachment, Laing considers to be most important. The task of psychotherapy is "the attempt of two people to recover the wholeness of being human through the relation between them."[36] The therapist's task is to appeal to what freedom remains to the imprisoned self, to enter into and understand his life and world, and further to encourage him to take the responsibility and the risk of choosing himself. Since the individual may prefer not to experience the "helplessness and bewilderment which would be the inevitable beginning of being himself,"[37] the therapeutic task is to coax this self from possibility into actuality, from nonbeing into being, from hiddenness into openness.

The goal is to "make contact with the original self of the individual" in which possibility we must believe, for the self is never completely destroyed.[38] The "I" may be unreal and encapsulated, but without the existence of such a residual self, therapy would be impossible. Laing's view of the unperishable core of the self reflects the understanding of the *imago Dei* of Kierkegaard.

The person himself, however, must take the risk of deciding whether the cure is worse than the disease. The individual may be able to break away from his original identification and create an identity for himself. But to break out from within the fantasy of the family system may be an act of suicide—the risk of defeat or madness. This process entails a hazardous contact with the unconscious fantasies that forces a complete reorientation of the self in its relation to others, although the means for doing so have been undermined by the fantasy system itself. The relation between this choice and the dread it entails is determined by the self's guilt. If the *inauthentic* guilt (i.e., guilt over *being* itself) can be overcome so that the *authentic* guilt (i.e., guilt over *not* being itself) breaks through, then the self may have been "educated by dread" to overcome dread.

Laing measures the authenticity of the self by a correspondence between the "person's position in relation to his actions."[39] It is a correspondence between the self's experience *and* its behavior rather than a division between them. When the self is "true" to itself, there would be no discrepancy between what the self says and what it means and does. Therefore, the self is transparent. When this occurs the doer is made real, authentic. (This is similar to Kierkegaard's understanding of truth as subjectivity in which there is a correspondence between the knower and what is known.)

The primary factor in unifying the self and healing the fundamental split between experience and behavior, Laing says, is the "physician's love, a love that recognizes the patient's total being and accepts it with no strings attached."[40] In other words, a final confirmation of the self which helps to dissolve its inauthentic guilt over being itself by way of acceptance is akin to "forgiveness," as Kierkegaard would put it. Laing's understanding of the imperishable core of the self, the "shred" that is not obliterated, that carries the possibility of freedom to change, to say "yes" to the self and to life, therein the hope of therapy lies.

Thus, the therapeutic goal is to intercept the dialectical movement of self-destruction, to win through to an affirmation of life rather than a negation of it. Therapy, therefore, provides a setting in which the self can take responsibility for becoming itself in the therapeutic milieu of "letting be"—the ultimate value for Laing. The schizoid self is terrified of love, for any form of understanding threatens his whole defense system. Yet he still wants to be understood and accepted for his true self by someone who will "let him be." Laing is close to Carl Jung in the belief that the schizophrenic ceases to be schizophrenic when he meets someone by whom he feels understood. The more the therapist is prepared to let him be, and is not engulfing him or treating him with indifference, the more hope there will be on the horizon.

Because of the terror that lies at the core of this condition, it is necessary that the therapist not "get too near too soon," Laing quotes Ludwig Binswanger as saying.[41] But finally it is the physician's love, a love that recognizes the patient's total being and accepts it, which is the main agent in uniting the patient. This love makes it possible to open the door to the real self. This real self, however, is not readily accessible not only because it feels unsafe, especially if exposed to being known, but also because it feels destructive. The therapist's role then is to be a target, against which rage can be directed, mistrust can be fought through in order to make possible self-revelation in place of self-encapsulation. By loving, the therapist helps to make whole.

Laing's later therapeutic suggestions seem no longer to rely on the principle of relatedness in the human mode of being. Rather, they recall the ancient quest for the self, the solitary journey into the self, the "dark night of the soul" of St. John of the Cross. Laing sees this as the possibility of a natural healing process. The self moves backward in order to move forward; the self explores inner space in order to recover itself. He sees it as a ceremonial initiation rather than the "degradation ceremonial of psychiatric examination."[42] For "breakdown" into this form of what is called "regression," in psychoanalytic terminology, might lead to a "breakthrough" to wholeness. This would mean a rebirth in which the ego would be relinquished for a transcendental experience of self. Laing would encourage this journey to the self's "lost home" and therefore writes, "If I could drive you out of your wretched mind, if I could tell you I would let you know."[43]

Laing would urge all of us to break through the "condition of alienation, of being asleep, of being unconscious, of being out of one's mind, which is the condition of the normal man,"[44] into an expanded and transformed consciousness. He claims that we have to go back a long way to contact the reality we have lost, back to where "the dreadful" happened, to regain our memory.

Laing describes the stages of the journey from outer to inner space into an entirely new environment as the oldest voyage of the world. It is the voyage from life to a kind of death, a death of the ego that the traveler may confuse with physical death, but that is a journey from the ego to the self. The journey into the loss of the self to gain the self is a descent into hell. But unless one has a "sheet anchor which helps . . . weather the storm,"[45] there is no assurance of return. The journey, in Laing's view, is not what we need to be cured of but is itself "a way of healing our own appalling state of alienation called normality."[46] Madness, Laing says, may not be all breakdown, it may also be breakthrough. It may also be a transcendental experience of the sort Laing believes to be the "original well spring of all religions."[47] In the state which we call sanity we experience ourselves and the world in the frame of reference of a consistent identity or what Laing refers to as the "egoic mode." But we must recognize, Laing argues, that "all religions and existential philosophies have agreed that such egoic experience is a preliminary illusion, a veil, a film of maya, a dream to Heraclitus and to Lao Tzu, the fundamental illusion of all Buddhism, a state of sleep, of death, of socially accepted madness, a womb state to which one has to die, from which one has to be born."[48] Self-encapsulation, narcissism, is what we must break through.

We will consider these comments in relation to Eastern religions in Chapter 5. As for our Western experience, I think we can say that ego loss or transcendental experience is illuminated with an inner light that burns and, often, consumes. There seems to be a positive correlation between lucidity and the depths of the unconscious plumbed. But since the return journey is not secured, lucidity can also be the fire that maddens and destroys (witness the lives of Friedrich Hölderlin and Nietzsche, among others). Our response to the alienated condition in which we find ourselves is therefore further self-encapsulation, further estrangement, an exaggerated individualism.

What we suffer from then is a cultural madness, a socially accepted madness. We live in "divided and distinguished worlds," Laing says, "in which experience is divorced from behavior. Sanity is equated with adaptation to external reality, and madness is correlated with entrance into an estranged internal reality. The outer, divorced from any illumination from the inner, is a state of darkness. We are in an age of darkness. The state of outer darkness is a state of sin, a state of alienation or estrangement from the *inner light.* "[49] To put out this light is sinful.

Transformation

The distinction that Laing made originally between the ontologically secure and the ontologically insecure has vanished. What he said originally of the schizoid individual he ultimately applies to everyman. We are all guilty of complicity in this, being subject to the human condition and members of the social order. In Laing's view, only by admitting our violence and recognizing that "we are as deeply afraid to live and to love as we are to die,"[50] can we begin to undo the violation of ourselves that has made it possible for us to live in a civilization "driven to its own destruction." He recommends for the divided, distinguished worlds of the social order the same therapy he recommends for the divided self. Rather than a sanity that has been madness, he urges madness that might lead to true sanity through death and rebirth with "a new kind of ego functioning, the ego now being a servant of the divine, no longer its betrayer."[51] Although we find ourselves threatened with destruction, no one knows what to do to stop it. Laing believes that there is one possible way out of our collusive madness—that vast "effort by modern society to flee from the self"[52]—We can attempt to understand our alienation from our selves and our experience, the split between our experience and our behavior. Given that we take this way out, it is just possible that a further transformation is possible.

The further transformation that Laing views as necessary, if men are to become whole, is not possible within the old clinical, medical model of what it is to be a person. According to the old view, psychiatry was concerned with mental illness. One looked for the cause in mind or body, environment, or heredity—depending on one's philosophical bias. A radical shift of outlook already has taken place in psychiatry in which old assumptions have been questioned. Laing explains that he does not use the term "schizophrenia" within this clinical frame of reference as Eugen Bleuler did, who coined it. Rather, he uses it to refer to a "label that some people pin on other people under certain *social circumstances,*" that is, where an interpersonal disjunction is occurring. The cause of schizophrenia is not to be found by examining the "patient" alone, but the whole social context in which the psychiatric ceremonial is set.[53] Laing indicates that a ceremonial social ritual is being conducted between psychiatrist and "patient" by means of which the "schizophrenic" is degraded as a human being by way of a theory that alienates us from our humanity, rather than being accepted, healed, and given a place as an individual in society. His point is that some individuals experience themselves and the world in ways incomprehensible to us and incongruent with our social norms.

It is this "existential and social" viewpoint which influences his conclusions regarding the nature of therapy. By way of making a distinction between clinical and existential psychiatric theory, Laing observes that one plane may be out of formation. That is the clinical view of schizophrenia. Or, from an ideal vantage point, it may become clear that the whole formation is off course. "If the formation itself is off course, then the man who is really to get 'on course' must leave the formation."[54] If our society is off course, if it may "have become biologically dysfunctional . . . [then] some forms of schizophrenic alienation from the alienation of society may have a sociobiological function that we have not recognized."[55]

Sin and Madness: Kierkegaard and Laing

We have asked about our strange condition, the schizophrenia of the human spirit. Man's pride, his self-concern, indeed the idolatry of self, has long been known to be fatal. We have considered a traditional understanding of sin through Kierkegaard's interpretation, and a modern understanding of madness through Laing's interpretation. What emerges from the juxtaposition of these views—a dialogue between sin and madness—is a possible response as to how it is that man "goes astray."

Sin and madness are ways of understanding man as a creature who flees from himself. Both Kierkegaard and Laing see man as a "mode of being which evades becoming." Laing sees the self in a dialectical relationship between being and nonbeing in which the self, confronted with the threat of nonbeing, attempts to preserve its being by paradoxically avoiding being itself. In an attempt to deal with the anxieties and dangers that threaten it, the self constructs a false self as a means of protecting its true self and thus it becomes a divided self. As a strategy for survival this effort is doomed—the self dies. Kierkegaard's understanding of the self is similar. He also perceives the self as existing in a dialectical relationship between being and nonbeing, for the self must choose "to be or not to be." The movement of the self is a transition from possibility to reality —from nonbeing to being, but in the face of dread. Dread lies at the crucial juncture of nonbeing and being. When the self refuses to be its "eternal" self, but chooses rather to be the self it wills to be, it thereby chooses nonbeing. Both Kierkegaard and Laing see this as a "tragic paradox" because the "more the self is defended this way, the more it is destroyed."[56]

For both Kierkegaard and Laing, the flight from the self is possible because the self is not an essence but an existential process. There is an assumption of the radical freedom of the self to be or not to be. Implicit in this freedom is the necessity to become itself. Decision is essential, as both Kierkegaard and Laing recognize, but as we have seen, it is precisely this about which the self is apprehensive. It fears being itself. In Kierkegaard's terms, in dread of being, the self "shuts itself up": divided from itself and its source, it suffers from the sickness unto death. In Laing's view, in terror of being, the self descends into nonbeing; it invents a strategy for survival—the strategy of self-division.

Laing's understanding of the ontological insecurity in which the "fall" occurs is similar to Kierkegaard's, despite the differences in their perspectives. The threat of annihilation is the occasion for the self's ontological insecurity. It is equally in dread of not being itself and of being itself, since that very being carries the possibility of nonbeing. The self is in the ambiguous situation of the "double bind"—which functions as the sympathetic antipathy of dread does in Kierkegaard's understanding. It both loves and fears "being able." In this situation the sickness manifests itself. In defending itself against the pain of life, the self has entered, Laing writes, the "condition called by Kierkegaard 'shutupness.' "[57]

For Kierkegaard this condition results from the inability to balance the factors of selfhood. The balance between distance and relation is implicitly necessary in Kierkegaard, as it is explicitly for Laing. But for Kierkegaard, distance and relation are seen in respect to God because the self exists in a balance between nearness to and farness from God. For Laing the ontological reality of the self lies in the self's relation to a "nexus of others." This dimension is conspicuously absent from Kierkegaard's writings. In fact, he rules out consideration of the relations with others except to warn against them. Kierkegaard perceived relations with others as an obstacle in the self's relation to God. Although Laing does not specify the source as God or speak of the realm of the eternal, he does insist that the self is radically estranged from the structure of being and alienated from its source—a state of sin, he says, for actions leading to estrangement used to be called sinful. With this, Kierkegaard would not argue—estrangement from oneself and from God is sin.

As Kierkegaard sees the self in the either/or predicament,

divided, in dread, between sin and faith, inauthenticity and authenticity, so Laing views the self as divided in a strategy for survival between false self and true self. Torn between nonbeing and being, according to Laing, the self goes astray in dread of being, as Kierkegaard said, because of the threat of annihilation. But, at this point, Laing qualifies and specifies what both have said. Therefore the self chooses to encapsulate itself in a false self—sin in Kierkegaard's terms, madness in Laing's—as a means of preserving its being and in its belief in its own destructiveness, "to preserve being from himself."[58] The self chooses "madness" in order *to be* at all. In dread, it is not possible not to "sin," the self is tied in "knots."

Sin has been traditionally located in pride, in self-idolatry, self-regard, or what is called narcissism. But what seems to emerge from an analysis of Kierkegaard's view of sin and Laing's view of madness—illuminated by the fate of Narcissus —is that what on the surface appears as pride or arrogant self-sufficiency is essentially a defensive mode of being, a defense in the face of dread and ontological insecurity against being oneself in which the will is bound in knots. Sin is corrupted will in the traditional view, freedom misunderstood and misused, but not simply that. It is not simply pride or narcissism in the usual sense of self-love. Rather, it is a defensive posture of self-absorption, self-preoccupation, because the self has been negated and is preoccupied with maintaining that negation in the defense of itself in order to preserve its being. The opposite of the sin of pride is faith—the acceptance of and willingness to be the self that one is. But, in dread, the self has "eyes that won't see" and "ears that won't hear," and a "heart that is hardened." Both Kierkegaard and Laing make it clear that the only outcome of this strategy is death-in-life. Both see this as the universal human condition. Sin and madness reflect the universal condition of narcissism—of self-encapsulation in which the self attempts to defend itself against the fate worse than death—the dread of being unloved and unloving. It does this by enclosing itself behind a mask of "self-love," under cover of which, however, is the corrosiveness of the "sickness unto death." Madness evokes what men have meant through the centuries when they have spoken in theological language of sin and the destructiveness of pride. Whether we speak of narcissism, or of the sin of pride, or of the divided self, we are concerned with a spiritual disorder of the individual and of mankind. This understanding of the flight from the self as madness and as sin and the resulting despair that issues from this state is a prior condition for its reversal. It is a call for a radical transformation of consciousness—*metanoia,* a total change of mind—which would mean the breaking of the shell of the old false self, the courage to drop the mask, a loss of the self to gain the self, death for there to be rebirth. Rather than a sanity that has been madness, we need a madness that might lead to a true sanity. For this we might give thanks, as for a special grace.

4

Sin and Madness:
A Transformation
of Consciousness

> Where did we go wrong? Where did our present habit of seeing
> the psychic isolation from what Teilhard de Chardin called
> "the divine milieu" begin to appear?
>
> *Harvey Cox*[1]

> Man abandoned is the manifestation of God as the one who
> abandons; man's forgetfulness of God is reflected in God's
> forgetfulness of man.
>
> *Paul Ricoeur*[2]

THE SICKNESS of the Spirit that is at the center of the psyche of man is clearly not new. The disorder from which Narcissus suffered is as old as man himself. It had its origins in our beginnings. Expressing the Biblical tradition, Kierkegaard understood it as the condition into which man "fell"—as sin. But we have undergone a transformation of consciousness. What was formerly thought of as sin is more readily understood now by what has become its equivalent: madness. Both sin and madness are linked at their core by narcissism—viewed as a strategy for survival. It is man's universal defense against recognition of his abandonment. We will consider now how man's relationship to existence has changed so as to make this strategy necessary. The way this pathology of self-consciousness has evolved—the estrangement of the self from itself and its source and self from other—can be seen clearly from the perspective of the transformation of our understanding of madness, as well as in relation to the traditional view of sin.

What the present age requires is a self-critical account of man, according to Laing. For humankind is estranged from its true potentialities. This means that we cannot assume an un-equivocal view about the sanity of ordinary common sense or about the madness of those so labeled.

We live "not only like other creatures in divers elements, but in divided and distinguished worlds."[3] What is required, then, is more than outcry and outrage; we must find out *how* it is that this has become so. We ask, What have we made of what we are? In other words, what have we done with our freedom? In a world that some have characterized as the age of the death of God, we might ask if what we have done with our freedom has not resulted in what might well be called the death of man. Is our heritage, then, not only the loss of God but also a corresponding loss of self?

Our contemporary despair, our estrangement from our-selves, from our world, and from God, was once called sin. By calling the Biblical tradition into question we have lost this tradition as one of the ways in which we have understood ourselves—as *imago Dei.* We have lost the category of sin as part of that understanding. Nietzsche was prophetic on this subject. He was "keenly aware of . . . the manner in which the non-existence of God would threaten human life with a com-plete loss of all significance," in fact, with madness.[4]

Laing agrees with this diagnosis of our condition: *"Deus absconditus.* Or we have absconded," he writes. He holds that our radical estrangement, the absence of presence, means mad-ness. He believes, however, that "the light had not faded. But between us and It, there is a veil which is more like fifty feet of concrete."[5] It is this wall we must blast through. The ab-sence of God is implicit in the loss of the self. And this es-trangement from God and self, what used to be called sin, is now considered to be madness.

Changes in Meaning

How is this so? What has happened? What is the change that has taken place and what is now meant by "madness"? Before we face this issue, let us first consider briefly why we should even ask such a question. What is the point of tracing such changes? What difference do they make? The point is that changes in the meaning of key words and phrases often reveal us to ourselves as individuals, but especially in respect to the structure of the social order. They are, Owen Barfield writes, "an important key to the history of the human mind and human civilization," a key to our social order, to its norms, and its deviations from them. The "norms . . . we call 'meanings' are involved in a constant process of change." In fact, "changes are made possible by . . . a discrepancy"[6] arising between the current usage or dictionary meaning and the meaning of a speaker who understands it in a new way. It can occur when there is already a discrepancy in meaning, as between two historical eras, and translation from the idiom of one into the idiom of the other opens up another way of understanding. The change can even amount to a complete about-face. We know that this has happened with the meaning of the word "subjective." Originally it meant "existing . . . in itself, or independently," whereas today it is used to signify just the opposite: "existing, if at all, only in someone's mind." There has been a similar reversal in respect to the meaning of the term "madness." "Progress involving change," Barfield believes, "does come about only when we question, and because we question, our fundamental assumptions. Moreover (and this is a crucial point . . .), the most fundamental assumptions of any age are those that are implicit in the meanings of its common words."[7]

Therefore, concentrating on the moment of change of meaning "awakens us to fundamental assumptions so deeply held that no one even thinks of making them explicit."[8] The point, then, in asking about a change in meaning, as I do here in respect to sin and madness, is to attempt to make explicit our fundamental assumptions, to make conscious our unconscious norms and models.

Changes in Human Consciousness

Now let us turn to the consideration of the question as to how we can account for such changes. Barfield suggests:

An important consideration that affects the history of any theory, and indeed, the history of ideas in general . . . [is that] there are two possible causes for people changing their ideas about anything as time goes on. One is that the thing has remained the same, but that people have come to think differently about it. . . . The other possible cause of a change of ideas is that the thing itself (that is, the kind of event) has changed in the meantime. . . . It is too often forgotten that, when it is changing ideas about human consciousness itself we are looking at, . . . the second cause is as likely to have predominated as the first. Ideas have changed because human consciousness itself—the elementary human experience about which the ideas are being formed —the whole relation between man and nature or between conscious man and unconscious man—has itself been in process of change.[9]

Self has undergone transformation in the course of its participation in the processes of the world. We come to be dealing with what Thomas Kuhn refers to as transformations of the "imagination in ways that we shall ultimately need to describe as a transformation of the world,"[10] or what L. L. Whyte calls "the changing structure of experienced and observed relationships."[11] For instance, in respect to the changing structure of experienced relationships, Laing notes:

Nowhere in the Bible is there any argument about the existence of gods, demons, angels. People did not first "believe in" God: they experienced His presence. . . . [But] . . . there have been profound changes in the experience of man. . . . Faith was never a matter of believing He existed, but of trusting in the presence that was experienced . . . as a self-validating datum.

Apparently, no such self-validating data are now experienced. Therefore, "we require a history of phenomena," he says, "not simply more phenomena of history."[12] Implicit in this is the view that the phenomenal world has changed along with the self because of the relationship inherent between the observer and that which is observed. In other words, consciousness, which is the reality of history, changes. What is now so clearly distinguished and divided into subject and object, self and not-self, inner and outer, conscious and unconscious, was not, presumably, always so. The self as we know it emerges ontogenetically, as it once did phylogenetically, from a relatively undifferentiated experiential matrix, in which self and not-self are not distinguished, separated, or distanced. As Martin Buber has said, "Man is the creature through whose being what is becomes detached from him and recognized for itself. Only when there is an independent opposite does a world exist."[13]

The splitting of experience into two aspects, one's awareness and the world of which one is aware, eventually leads to our dualistic mode of thought, to divided and distinguished worlds. Furthermore, the connection of the self with the not-self has become unconscious. This is now a crucial aspect of our contemporary despair. This estrangement is relatively recent. The dualistic detachment reached its peak in the seventeenth century with René Descartes, in whose thought it is epitomized. In splitting the classical correspondence between microcosm and macrocosm, Descartes removed any spiritual principle from reality and divided man and world. He found reality as thought to be within the ego; the world of extension was de-godded, de-spirited, and turned over as object to science. The self has become estranged from reality to the point of derangement. An "unholy madness," Norman Brown has called it. It seems small wonder then, as Barfield comments, that a generation so alienated "developed a sympathetic response to the psycho-analytical gnosis of dream-imagery, and [readily] accepted the . . . idea of an immaterial realm of 'the unconscious.' "[14] The unconscious is, after all, perhaps the only route back into that estranged reality. Whyte points out that the development of the idea of the unconscious between 1680 and 1860 was a corrective to the overemphasis in the century before on the rational consciousness of the individual. He notes, "It is only after Descartes that we find first the idea and then the term 'unconscious mind' entering European thought."[15]

This transition from immediate awareness of the phenomenal world to a consciousness of self as subject and preoccupation with the phenomenal world as object represents a change in the data of experience. If we look at the process of change in the relation of conscious and unconscious self, we find, as Barfield suggests, that "as soon as unconscious . . . processes have been sufficiently polarized" to detach the self from world, man from nature, inner from outer, subject from object, they give rise to the phenomenal world, on the one hand, and to self-consciousness, on the other. Thus "memory is made possible." Likewise a history of which we can be aware is made possible, for "the remembered phenomena become detached or liberated from their originals and so, as images, are in some measure at man's disposal."[16] In Whyte's view, the sharp separation of subject from object—first intuitively and later in rational analysis—was not perverse, but a necessary stage toward a fuller realization of the human intellect. Detachment of self and world, on the one hand, has brought about the alienation of the self to the degree that we can speak of madness and of the existential death of man. But, on the other hand, it spells freedom. Modern self-consciousness has come into being along with a historical sense. According to Barfield, "it is only when detachment has progressed to a certain point that man becomes able to observe the changes which constitute history." It is only when "he begins to observe them that he becomes fully conscious of himself."[17] Detachment, therefore, has made possible the conscious historical remembering by means of which we may, if we will, again incorporate in some transformed fashion the estranged reality.

Our task, then, and the function of history may be to undertake this re-membering by way of imaginative reconstruction of the forgotten phenomena. This would be what Whyte calls therapeutic history. The function of history would then be what Freud prescribed for the individual psyche, to turn the unconscious into memory. It is memory understood as historical consciousness, not so-called objective truth, which shall make us free. For since it presupposes distance and implies the emergence of the self from the unconscious past, it also means release from the bonds of unconscious will. On the social level, it means deliverance from the repetition compulsion in the movement of history.

With this view of the evolution of consciousness in mind, let us return to our question. How is it that what was previously thought of as sin now comes to be considered as madness? The change is well summed up in a revealing anecdote. In 1969, the dean of a Catholic university remarked about the organization called WITCHES: "A couple of hundred years ago, we would have burned them at the stake. Twenty-five years ago, I would have expelled them. Now we simply send them all to psychiatrists."

There we have it. Referring to the changing character of madness, Laing has said concerning the late fifteenth-century tract *Malleus Maleficarum* (the Witches' Hammer)[18] that the Inquisition concerned itself with problems that we regard today as being in the domain of psychiatry. They thought that these problems were caused by black magic practices on the sufferer. If someone claims now that black magic is being practiced on him, he is considered to be mad. His belief would be treated as a symptom for which a psychiatrist might prescribe a pharmacological remedy. If the Inquisition's therapeutic ideology, its demonology, were now regarded as psychotic, might not the naturalistic psychiatric thought also be a delusional system, culturally sanctioned? To understand what lies behind our emerging notion of madness, and its relation to our earlier understanding of sin, we must trace its history not as a series of events, but rather as a changing "world view" against the background of the fundamental experience of man from what we might call immediacy to detachment.

From Sin to Madness: Divine Madness

The first understanding of madness apparently stemmed from a world outlook quite different from ours. It was similar to the understanding of inspiration, as the breathing into man of the divine spirit. It was like "the doctrine of mania," as Barfield described it, "or divine madness, of *enthousiasmos*, of possession by a god."[19] It was an invasion of the self by a spirit other than one's own ego. This psychology persisted into the Renaissance, when self-consciousness emerged into full bloom. Earlier, what self-awareness there was, was sporadic and transitory in an otherwise undifferentiated realm of experience. Given that outlook, in contrast with ours today, there was really nothing so remarkable in the ancients' view that what we would refer to as supersensible reality could directly affect and influence their minds and bodies. Under such circumstances, certainly, the self could be invaded by a spirit other than the individual's own. Ideas were divine ideas taken in by men, and madness was divine also, possession by a god.

In the Old Testament, for instance, a prophetic revelation was seen as coming through the mediation of personal consciousness but was not personal. In our clear distinction between the objective and subjective, hearing a voice would mean some individual aberration, but that was not so in the Israelite community for whom God was the source of prophetic revelation. Prophecy was essentially ecstatic in character, an instance of the psychology of inspiration. The "prophetic spirit was not in the prophet," but rather "it was the spirit, the word, or the hand of the Lord, that came upon him or took hold of him."[20] The prophets spoke not their own words, but those of the Lord. In fact, the test of a true prophet could be said to be his teaching of trust in the Lord rather than in anything else— certainly not in himself. The significant point is that the prophet's personal experience of God was not a private matter, nor was it understood as the working of an individual psyche. His message was, rather, an element in the continuing dialogue between God and man, which was experienced as inspiration.

Possession, trance (ecstatic states), and related phenomena were accepted as socially significant within the framework of the Israelite community. This point is important for an understanding of the limits within which the society viewed deviant behavior as socially acceptable, and which thus also defined the boundaries of what was considered mad. In other words, the society establishes its "range" by its understanding of "derangement," to use Michel Foucault's terms. If prophecy was considered madness (there is evidence in the roots of words that connect terms meaning frenzy, out of one's senses, deranged, and acting like a prophet), it was nevertheless regarded as divinely inspired. It is evidence of the cultural relativity of madness that Karl Jaspers attempted to show that Ezekiel, who was subject to frenzies and states of trance, was a schizophrenic. But such a procedure, looking back into the past by way of our current medical categories, issues from the current absolute division between madness and nonmadness. It assumes that the object we are trying to understand is static, while only our understanding has become more accurate and complete. Actually the kind of event may have changed. Being-taken-hold-of-by-God, as experienced by the prophets, was certainly of another order and manifested a very different world view from ours, in which we understand madness as pathology, or the hell of an isolated private world. From the viewpoint of a post-Cartesian culture, it may be considered desirable to have a rationalistic explanation of these acts. Nevertheless, an interpretation in terms of conscious rational action is inadequate. An explanation of possession, trance, and other shamanistic behavior associated with these states solely in terms of psychopathology is untenable. Behavior that would be regarded as psychotic in our culture may be highly valued and have a useful social role in another. The psychopathology of those who are different, it would seem, is more a judgment of the way their position is interpreted by that society than of their personality structure per se. These are considerations we should remember when trying to define and draw distinctions between sanity and madness.

Possession, the divine madness, was an accepted way of understanding, and a normal means of establishing relations with supernatural or superindividual powers in the Greek world as well. Invasion by a god was understood to result in a madness characterized by raving and frenzied behavior, a state of ecstatic excitement similar to the behavior of the Old Testament prophets when they prophesied. It was believed that a god such as Dionysus, Apollo, Aphrodite, or the Muses—those listed by Socrates in his four divisions of madness—could enter the individual so that he would become *entheos,* having the god in him, being one with the god. It is this state of madness that Plato associates with divine inspiration and its blessings, for no one, according to Plato, achieves inspiration and prophetic truth when in his right mind. It is necessary that the mind should first have lost its workaday consciousness and be "possessed." Socrates points out in the *Phaedrus* that madness is a divine gift and the source of the chief blessings granted to men. For prophecy is a madness, he says, and points out that the word for prophecy and the one for madness differ by only one letter. Since they are called by the same name, he concludes that "there was an inspired madness which was a noble thing," and "superior to a sane mind, for the one is only of human, but the other of divine origin" (*Phaedrus,* 49).

Madness as Demonic Possession

By the Middle Ages, concepts of madness, derived from the ideas of classical antiquity, were changed and modified. Possession was looked upon primarily as demonic, a manifestation of the devil, and therefore as possession by sin. Until the eighteenth century, madness, no longer holy, was subsumed under the category of sin. "In the Middle Ages and until the Renaissance," Michel Foucault tells us, "man's dispute with madness was a dramatic debate in which he confronted the secret powers of the world; the experience of madness was clouded by images of the Fall and the will of God."[21]

Consciousness of Satan and of his powers was carried to a

new height during the twelfth and thirteenth centuries. For almost three centuries, during the waning Middle Ages, Europe swarmed with "witches" possessed by the devil. It was not until the end of the eighteenth century that executions for witchcraft ceased in Europe. There have been varying explanations of the phenomenon. According to George Rosen,[22] witch-hunting expresses a dis-ease of society and is related to its social context. By the end of the Middle Ages the old order was dying away and the medieval soul, held by various sorts of occult ties to the physical body and to the world, was beginning to be torn away from these bonds. Paul Tillich referred to the pre-Reformation era as one "which deserves the name of the 'age of anxiety.' "[23]

But it is hard for us to understand the demonology of the Inquisition, for from our viewpoint, as Laing noted, that agency dealt with a number of problems which would be regarded today as psychiatric matters. But, as we read in the *Malleus,* the causes of these difficulties were found by the Inquisitors in Germany to be traceable to activities of the devil, to witchcraft, and to the practice of black magic. As Laing has pointed out, if a naturalistic explanation had been offered, it would have been considered heretical or worse. Madness was demonic possession, and this state of corruption was possible only if the individual affected was a grave sinner. If the world was indeed disintegrating, as many believed, then it was thought that perhaps to purge it of sin would help to restore it. This required a battle against Satan, the source of sin and evil. In the struggle against Satan an elaborate ideology was constructed and acted upon by the Inquisition in Germany. Fear of demonic powers was widespread throughout the later Middle Ages and underpinned the demonology readily accepted by all. The devil, and thereby sin, could be attacked by way of his agents, the witches who were possessed by him.

Tillich points out that "death and the devil were allied in the anxious imagination"[24] of the late Middle Ages. According to Foucault, the theme of madness was substituted for that of death but did not really mark a break with it. It was, rather, another aspect of it. What was in question was still the nothingness at the core of existence, so that now madness was denounced everywhere, for madness announced the end of the world. Madness fascinated the Middle Ages, as we can tell from the fantastic images appearing in both graphic and literary forms. The fascination of madness was the fascination of knowledge, but knowledge is associated with the devil and the injunction not to eat of the forbidden tree. Therefore this forbidden wisdom implies the victory of Satan and doomsday, that is, death and nothingness.

By the end of the fifteenth century, mockery of madness replaces the theme of death and nothingness. Madness, as folly, wears a foolscap. *"La folie"* was a major theme, and a whole list of follies attributed to a vague sort of unreason appeared. It was, Foucault writes, "as if that world, whose network of spiritual meanings was so closeknit, had begun to unravel, showing faces whose meaning was no longer clear except in the forms of madness."[25]

In this unraveling of the ancient web of spiritual meaning, we see something closer to our understanding of the individual spirit, or spirit as possessed by the isolated individual, coming to light. Note, for instance, the image of Folly, which loomed large at the end of the Middle Ages, as we find her in Erasmus' *Praise of Folly.* Folly is to be beside oneself, as Johan Huizinga explains in his comments on Erasmus' work,[26] and when are we beside ourselves? When the spirit breaks its fetters and tries to escape from its prison and aspires to liberty. That is madness, he says, but it is also otherworldliness—the highest wisdom. Madness, in the form of Folly, is interpreted not as *in*spired by the god but as *as*piring outward toward the otherworldly.

The Light of Reason: Unholy Madness

Beginning with the seventeenth century, madness no longer had much instructive value. The great theme of madness began to disappear; forbidden wisdom became forgotten wisdom.

With the erosion of belief in the spiritual fabric, which had encompassed man's life, an individual psychology was beginning to emerge. Self-consciousness as we know it seems to have dawned in Europe about this time. Parallel with this detachment of the self from the world, the "light of reason" began to clear away the darkness of demonology and demonological categories. At this point, madness changed its meaning. Whereas before this madness was inspired—was, in fact, possession by a spirit, either benevolent or malevolent—now scientific biological categories begin to appear. Medieval views of madness begin to give way to medical categories by means of which, it was believed, madness could be rationally understood and therefore mastered, which allayed the fear of demonic powers. With this development the category of sin in relation to madness began to fade away and pretty well disappeared in the Enlightenment. An increasingly naturalistic view of madness emerged, a view that is still dominant today. The experiences described as possession and trance, for example, are now characterized in psychiatric terms as dissociative states, that is, states in which there is, as Rosen puts it, a "division of consciousness with a segregation of mental processes and ideas, to such an extent that they function as unitary wholes as if belonging to another person."[27]

Madness is no longer understood as a manifestation of spirit; consciousness is divided. Foucault points to the period from Thomas Willis (1621–1675) to Philippe Pinel (1745–1826), from Racine to de Sade and Goya, as the era in which the relation between madness and reason changed, as the realm preceding complete division of madness and reason, in which their dialogue was broken. Madness in this epoch no longer signified another world, and there was no place for it in the social order. It has been generally held that William Tuke (1732–1822) and Pinel were the saviors of the mentally ill, but the truth of the matter, Foucault tells us, is not so simple:

The legends of Pinel and Tuke transmit mythical values, which nineteenth century psychiatry would accept as obvious in nature. But, beneath the myths themselves, there was an operation . . . which silently organized the world of the asylum, the methods of cure and, at the same time, the concrete experience of madness.

In fact, in the asylum which Tuke created, "where he substituted for the free terror of madness the stifling anguish of responsibility, fear . . . now raged under the seals of conscience."[28]

Pinel advocated a moral context for the asylum but actually put it in a purely medical framework. Religious opinions were used in the service of medicine in order to effect a cure, but the asylum was a realm without religion, where morality and ethical uniformity reigned. Madness was treated as arrogance rather than aberration. Foucault concludes that

from Pinel on, madness would be regarded as an impulse from the depths which . . . tends to an apotheosis of the self. For the nineteenth century, the initial model of madness would be to believe oneself to be God, while for the preceding centuries it had been to deny God.[29]

The asylum of the age of positivism, founded by Pinel, was not simply a place for diagnosis and therapy. It was, rather, that institution in which one was judged, accused, and condemned. Madness was to be punished in the asylum, even though it was guiltless outside of it. Even in our own day it is imprisoned in a world of morality.

The transformation of madness into mental illness, at the end of the eighteenth century, is evidence of the broken dialogue between madness and nonmadness. The science and language of psychiatry, within which reason conducts a monologue about madness, was grounded in that broken dialogue, that silence. Foucault predicts, "Madness will never again be able to speak the language of reason, with all that in it transcends the natural phenomena of disease. It will be entirely enclosed in pathology."[30]

This metamorphosis, in which madness becomes disease, occurred when slowly . . . the eighteenth century constituted, around its awareness of madness and of its threatening spread, a whole new order of concepts. In the landscape of unreason where the sixteenth century had located it, madness concealed a meaning and an origin that were . . . related to sin. . . . In the second half of the eighteenth century, madness was no longer recognized in what brings man closer to an immemorial fall. . . . It was, on the contrary, situated in those distances man takes in regard to himself, to his world, to all that is offered by the immediacy of nature; madness (seen as disease) became possible in that milieu where man's relations with his feelings, with time, with others, are altered; madness (unholy) was possible because of everything which in man's life and development is a break with the Fall, but of a new order, in which men begin to have a presentiment of history, and where there formed, in an obscure originating relationship, the "alienation" of the physicians and the "alienation" of the philosophers—two configurations in which man in any case corrupts his truth.[31]

Madness as Correlative to Sin

But it is precisely in this alienation, in this corruption of man's truth, that what we have always known as sin lies. And it is this understanding of our madness—as of the "order of the Fall," that is, of sin—that I believe we find emerging. During the course of human history, from Socrates' divine madness to Pinel's disease of madness, from holy to unholy madness, our experience of madness has clearly been changing. In fact, it has undergone an inversion correlative with the change in human consciousness itself; that is, the change in the relationship between the conscious and the unconscious, between self and world. The data of experience—our perceptions and our interpretations of them—about which our ideas have been formed have been in a process of change, and this is reflected in our shifting understanding of madness. In this transformation of consciousness, there has been an actual transition from one kind of event to another kind. It can be seen as the transition from the being-taken-hold-of by something, by some force or being, some element of not-self, conceivable when the self is in intimate relation to the surrounding matrix, to a taking-hold-of something conceivable now when the self as subject and the surrounding matrix as object are divided and separated. Madness, once understood as being possessed by a demon or a god, came to be regarded as what the individual madman himself actively possessed as an objective, measurable entity, a disease. A view is now emerging, it seems, which regards madness in another way: as a further transformation of the kind of event taking place. It regards it as a transition from a mode of being of willingness to be possessed by a god or demon, to a mode of being that can be described as a willed position, and, according to Laing, as a strategy devised for survival.

In accord with this emerging view of madness, the myth of disease is gradually and with difficulty being dispelled. "To be mad," Laing says, "is not necessarily to be ill, notwithstanding that in our culture the two categories have become confused."[32] For Laing, what appears to be illness, breakdown, is the possibility of breakthrough. On the other hand, the pathology, the disorder, is looked upon as disorder of the spirit. It is, on one level, a massive derangement in which we find that the range of our consciousness has been reduced over the ages and has thus become constricted to the point where it has become a pathology of self-consciousness. This pathology involves a separation from, and unconsciousness of, the center and source of our existence. It is this estrangement from reality that Laing calls pseudo sanity, which is mad and maddening. He points out, citing Heidegger, that "the Dreadful has already happened"—a phrase suggestive of the Fall and the consequent brokenness of existence—and, Laing says,

if you split Being down the middle, if you insist on grabbing this without that, if you cling to the good without the bad, denying the one from the other, what happens is that the dissociated evil impulse, now evil in a double sense, returns to permeate and possess the good and turn it into itself.[33]

This is what we have known, in the language of sin, as the rebellion against the given or true self—the refusal to be one's self, as Søren Kierkegaard saw it. Rather than willing to be the self that it is, the self wills to construct itself. Translated into the twentieth-century language of phenomenological depth psychology, we find that this disorder of the spirit, which is at the center of the sickness of the psyche, understood as madness, has become the equivalent of what has been understood as sin. It is this universal condition of the corruption of man's truth of which Laing speaks. Instead of having what Blake called double vision—a vision that is informed by both sides of consciousness—we have a divided vision, a split consciousness; we have false selves; experience is divorced from behavior, and, with experience violated, we become violent. "If our experience is destroyed," Laing writes, "we have lost our own selves." The result, as Pascal said, is that "men are so necessarily mad, that not to be mad would amount to another form of madness."

This could be otherwise, Laing emphasizes:

Psychiatry could be on the side of transcendence, of genuine freedom and of true human growth, [instead of being] a technique of inducing behavior that is adjusted. . . . [For] our normal adjusted state is too often the abdication of ecstasy (once considered divine) and the betrayal of our true potentialities, [so that] many of us are only too successful in acquiring a false self to adjust to false realities.[34]

The change in meaning of madness points to the possibility of a new understanding, to the possibility of a new attempt to reintegrate the estranged reality, to see that subject and object are related. The emergence of phenomenological psychology asks that we recognize again the relationship between observer and observed, as well as the inextricable connection between self and world.

Concomitant with the transformation of our consciousness, there has been a change in the possible forms of our understanding. For with the loss of God and the questioning of the traditional Biblical understanding of man as *imago Dei*, as well as the questioning of the traditional Greek belief in the correspondence between rationality and reality and man as rational being—in other words, with the disintegration of the two fundamental strands of Western culture—we have lost the two major ways of understanding ourselves. Our understanding, however, may well have been transposed and cast in a new form. The Biblical mythos that has ordered our understanding would seem to be in the process of being transposed into a new idiom. The category of sin may, for many, be no longer viable, but, in its equivalent understanding, the category of madness carries its implications and weight: estrangement from Source and self is the meaning of both. Although *imago Dei* may no longer seem a viable way of self-understanding, it would appear that Laing's view of madness, within which is implicit an essential possibility of the self that it is not, a true self buried in the false self adjusted to false realities, speaks of that very doctrine.

The Possibility of a New Mythos

It is possible that we can now understand ourselves and our predicament by understanding madness—madness, which curiously invokes both the devil of the Biblical tradition and the divine madness of the Greek tradition, and may perhaps fuse them both. Our real choice may be between holy and unholy madness—a choice between the divine madness, *entheos,* and the madness of the devil, the madness of estrangement and death. Laing tells us that what appears as madness is a pseudo madness, as the sanity of the constructed self is pseudo sanity. The therapeutic method of madness that he suggests is rooted in the ancient tradition of the spiritual journey, a dangerous and ambiguous quest, which has always meant a descent into the depths of hell, into the dominion of the devil, there to encounter and overcome the obscure forces of dread, of demons and dangers, in order to seek, and return with, the treasure of life, a death and rebirth, a transformed consciousness —*metanoia*—a loss of the self to receive the self. Madness, then, would be seen to function dialectically as both sickness of spirit and essential for cure. So it is with dread and despair

—that is, sin, according to Kierkegaard—for despair is that dangerous sickness of the spirit which it is essential to suffer for there to be cure. Despair in the language of sin, madness in the idiom of phenomenological psychology, are required for reversal. This pseudo madness, Laing believes, is the possibility of true sanity, for when the center will no longer hold, when the will can no longer will the mask of the false self, then that failure of the will becomes the possibility of the breakthrough of the alienated spontaneous self. Therefore Laing's cry that, if he "could drive you out of your mind," in other words, out of the alienation of duality, he would do so. But this radical method is not, as Laing agrees, for everyone.

Therapeutic History

It is at this point that we return to our beginning, to the function of history. For history, seen as a way of restoring our consciousness, could be for all of us. If this madness, in which we are all implicated, is deranged experience and detached behavior based on intentional forgetting of what is the totality of the case, and obsessive attachment to a partial reality, and if the function of history is understood as a re-membrance, as the turning into memory of this wisdom—wisdom re-membered—the estranged reality might be re-integrated and re-possessed. Memory makes the restoration of the will possible, for the split-off experience, the unconscious fantasies that are organizing our experience, are functioning autonomously as unconscious will. And the will is bound in the past. The locus of the problem is—as Augustine and Luther, Pascal and Kierkegaard, knew and as Laing now tells us—the bondage of the will. The old problem of the will as the root of sin, and now of madness, dormant for centuries, has again emerged, although now as unconscious will bound in unconscious fantasies, a position taken, a pattern followed, by the unconscious will divided from and in conflict with conscious intention.

To heal the breach, which has widened into madness, would mean to uncover, to make conscious, this unconscious intention—we might say this world view—which forms and informs the self's experience and behavior. This reconstruction of memory might in turn make possible the rearrangement of the relationships within the fantasy that is functioning as paradigm. The restructured experience reconstructs the will, the self's dominant intention. Therefore, when we remember our memory, we are at the same time making it possible to remember our will. Memory is the antidote to the repetition compulsion, the unconscious willing to re-experience and re-enact the original paradigmatic situation. It would seem to heal the divided will by making possible the coincidence of conscious and unconscious intention, of spontaneous impulse and voluntary purpose. And that is the possibility of freedom, the self at rest in motion, as Augustine put it. This remembrance might even be seen as a contemporary form of holy madness, now imaginatively directed to repossess what has been estranged and forgotten, instead of being possessed by it. This would be *metanoia*, indeed, a madness whose truth might lead to a true sanity rather than to a sanity whose falseness has been madness.

Western thought has been clear, and systematically so, about the human predicament, elaborating it in both its sacred and secular literature—in the context of sin and of madness. In the East, there is not the dichotomy between sacred and secular in their literature as there is in the West, nor do we find sin and madness stated or described as such. However, what we do find points to the same fundamental human reality clothed in different forms.

5

Neither Sin nor Madness: Eastern Equivalents

> [In Hindu philosophy] . . . the primary concern . . . has always been, not information, but transformation; a radical changing of man's nature . . . a renovation of his understanding both of the outer world and of his own existence; a transformation . . . such as will amount when successful to a total conversion or rebirth.
>
> *Heinrich Zimmer*[1]

> Buddhism and Biblical Christianity agree . . . man is somehow not in his right relation to the world . . . man bears in himself a mysterious tendency to falsify that relation. . . . This falsification is what Buddhists call *Avidya*. *Avidya* . . . "ignorance" . . . is an invincible error. . . . It is a disposition to treat the ego as an absolute.
>
> *Thomas Merton*[2]

> Other echoes
> Inhabit the garden. Shall we follow?
>
> *T. S. Eliot*[3]

WHEREVER WE TURN, we are taught the same lesson, which is that when man is separated from his Source, feeling abandoned, loveless, and in exile, he defends himself against the recognition of this condition in self-destructive ways. This view of narcissistic man is not unique to Western thought, but is plainly evident in the literature of the Eastern religions as well —despite significant differences in their perspectives[4] on the nature of reality and man's essential relationship to it.

What is the Eastern response to man's predicament? What does Eastern wisdom tell us about man's condition? In very broad terms, it tells us that what we in the West refer to as

pride and which we have written of as narcissism, self-centeredness, self-encapsulation, is ignorance *(avidyā)*. In ignorance,
man suffers from an egocentric consciousness. As Kierkegaard
said in his way and Laing in his, the Eastern traditions also
consider egoic experience an illusion, a veil of maya, in short,
they tell us that self-enclosure, narcissism, is madness, that our
hyperindividualism is madness. It is that wall they also attempt,
by means of rigorous spiritual disciplines, to scale.

In the West, abandoned, we developed mastery and self-
sufficiency, individualism and technology. In the East—and we
shall further define these generalizations when we look at the
sacred literature of each religion—the recognition of man's
condition and the diagnosis are similar to those of the West.

What is sought in the East is not personal relatedness to
other or to God, the tensive polarity between separation and
attachment advised by the Western tradition,[5] but rather
reunion, the recognition of the identity of self. All, to overcome man's separation. We shall now look more closely at the
major Eastern religions to understand how their views of the
human condition reflect the image of Narcissus.

Hinduism

Let us first consider the broad and diversified religious tradition known as the Hindu tradition—a tradition so complex
that generalizing and concluding that there is an essence of
Indian religion, of course, falsifies it. But, with that caveat in
mind, we must try to extract some general truths.

Hinduism is the name given to a family of religions—the
living faith of the peoples of India.[6] The Hindu tradition finds
the physical and material world secondary to the reality of
mind and spirit. The natural world is seen as an obstacle to
gaining that reality. The Hinduism portrayed in the early Vedic literature is a this-worldly religion, but, ultimately, in the
later Brahmanic and Vedantic literature it became otherworldly. Whereas we find it hard to believe much in inner or
unseen reality, Hindus find it hard to put much store in mate-

rial reality. The phenomenal world is a veil of illusions and deception (as Laing has said). Deliverance from this realm of maya, of materiality, is the goal of life. The present, immediate world of now is rejected. The eternal and ultimate are sought. Deliverance from the realm of maya and *union* with ultimate reality is what is sought. It is precisely the reality of the invisible and inner as contrasted with the visible and material that it is so difficult for most Westerners to understand. It may help us to recall the Platonic view that reality and truth are hidden, or at best, inadequately revealed in the visible world as shadows of the real.

By and large, Hinduism holds that man's predicament—the human condition—is the result of wrong thought, of igno rance. It is an ignorance of the truth of the invisible ultimate reality and of the falseness of what appears to be real, that is man's *apparent* separation from the real. Therefore, the Hin dus contend that miseries do not arise from sin as it is under stood in Western thought but rather with a fallacious under standing of reality and appearance.

In recognition of the significance of the reality of the invisi ble and inner world, Hinduism emphasizes a quest for libera tion from the phenomenal world, a cultivation of the inner or true self—which is reality—and its release from the empirical self. This release culminates in salvation: a mystical union between the self and the ultimate reality, the cosmic reality. The individual self, or Atman, is one with the universal self or Brahman. Ignorance of this psycho spiritual unity is at the root of man's suffering. Knowledge of it—*realized* knowledge —is liberation. In the West such knowledge, such identifica tion with the cosmic spirit, would be seen perhaps as mysticism —at best, as odd; at worst, as psychotic. Yet the Hindu term for the sacred literature is *veda*, which means "knowledge," and, interestingly, it is linguistically related to the English *wisdom* and the German *wissen*—which mean "to know."

What is it we are to know? What is saving knowledge? That Atman/Brahman is one. Separation is unreality. This is not an ethical conception but an ontological one. It is the notion that man participates in reality and that *what is*—the truth—ought to be known. The Hindus emphasize the coincidence of being and knowing, truth and knowledge. The Hindu response to man's narcissism (that is, his self-concern, which is generated by his separation) is self-transcendence by way of unity with ultimate reality. Eastern thought turns to "attachment" rather than to mastery and self-sufficiency in the face of separation as we in the West have done. In Hindu thought man need not be self-concerned, self-preoccupied, or self-idolatrous, for he is securely anchored, if not visibly then invisibly, in reality. Man can know that "what appears" is not the whole of reality. This distinction, which originates in the early Vedic religious ritual, was developed in the later Upanishads as the basis for the *identification.* This identification of self and cosmos is how Hinduism addresses itself to man's narcissism—his tendency to make his individual self the ultimate reality—in the face of the dread of freedom and abandonment in these "infinite spaces." In the early Vedas it was assumed that immortality—a return of the self to the Self—once gained, was a permanent state. In the later Brahmanas, the fear arose that even this state was not free from death, from separation. It was feared that the effects of past ritual actions, assuring one's immortality, which meant release from earthly suffering, would run out and death and separation once again occur. This re-death was a *dreadful* prospect. The once-secure universe no longer seemed to be so. Unity was not a permanent thing. It was in this way that the conclusion was gradually reached—over centuries and strata of Vedic literature—that the phenomenal world might in the end be one in which man, no less than the rest of nature, was caught up in a continuing cycle of creation and of destruction. And, if this was so, then what was the value of a perhaps longer lasting but ultimately impermanent afterlife—an ultimately impermanent union with reality?

A new understanding of man was needed to meet these concerns since earlier Vedic tradition had paid little attention to it. The ritually based Brahmanical world view saw the phenomenal world as a creation brought forth by the magic of ritual, which was conceived as the central support of the universe. But the effectiveness of the ritual itself began to be questioned because if not only death but re-death brought an end to its benefits, the effects of past rituals action might run out and be impermanent. If this was so, then the whole Brahmanical system was called into question. Was there then some higher goal, some true state of immortality that was not ruled by death and could not be eroded by time? If so, how might it be obtained? How could man transcend his condition of ignorance?

It is to these questions that the Indian religious tradition addressed itself, and the answers to these questions constitute the search for the self of man. It was generally assumed in the Brahmanas that proper ritual action was as important as proper knowledge. At times, however, the Brahmanas claimed that knowledge alone would bring the desired result, without ritual actions. By the end of the Brahmanic period, about 800 B.C., the independent effect of this ritual knowledge was widely acknowledged. The concept of the ritual was extended to include mental as well as physical performance, in the belief that ritual sounds and actions could be internalized or converted into thought, without a loss of power. This knowledge was passed down as restricted or secret teachings in the collections called Aranyakas, the forest books, because their contents were taught and put into practice in forest retreats. The Aranyakas thus gave a new status to the individual person. Knowledge, though derived from the sacrificial ritual, did not depend for its effectiveness on the elaborate rituals of the sacrifice. Mental ritual performance could bring the same results. The performer was thus raised in power and importance to the level of the sacrifice itself. A person of advanced training and knowledge became a creator in his own right. Like the Brahmin priest, he could meditate on the meaning of the sacrifice, search out its hidden truth, and control the universe by the power of his mantras, the verses of the Vedas, indeed by the power of his mantras alone.

This development led to a conclusion that was only slowly

recognized. If the individual person had the power of the sacrifice, then in the most basic sense he *was* the sacrifice. He thus became, like Perusa, the creator god, who brought the world into creation by way of his own sacrifice. The individual could be both the sacrifice and the sacrificer. In this way phenomenal man could be conceived of as an extension of his own inner nature, his own essential self.

But what *was* the essential self of man? The term introduced into Vedic inquiry was the common word for self, *ātman*. Atman was the inner self, the principle that constituted man's essential nature. Throughout the Vedic period many suggestions were made as to what the nature of that self might be. The most important suggestions, however, focused on the concept of Brahman. Brahman was treated as *the* basic cosmic principle. Brahman is understood not only as the basic principle of cosmos but it is also the self of man. Brahman is the sustaining power or reality behind the universe. Now the person who knows this Brahman as his Atman, or self, has no need to fear for his being, because his Atman, or self, participates in eternal cosmic reality.

The attempt to understand Brahman as the reality of both man and the cosmos led to investigation of human experience in order to describe the self in empirical or phenomenal terms. This investigation is the central theme of the last group of Vedic writings, the Upanishads. The knowledge that the self requires is not that ignorance of the identity of Brahman and Atman is the problem, but an actual elimination of the ignorance. *Saving knowledge* is knowledge that is *lived* in every thought and action. A person with such knowledge is *transformed.* Indeed, he must be transformed in order to have such knowledge. How can the self achieve this knowledge and so be released from bondage to the empirical self? Release can be effected only by knowledge that counteracts the self-perpetuation of the phenomenal self. And that knowledge is that the true self *is* Brahman. If one really knows this experientially, then there is no purpose in maintaining an isolated individual existence. The ignorance of the self falls away when saving knowledge is personally appropriated and the phenomenal self then terminates its existence when the body dies. The goal of man is, then, to dissolve the empirical, phenomenal, or subtle self and so to be released from rebirth. Hence, a person who chose to ignore the inner self and rested content with the natural world was acting ignorantly in a way that could only result in illusion and suffering and a continuation of bondage to the cycle of endless rebirth.

Therefore, although ritual sacrifices as a means of altering the natural world might have some merit in improving one's life, salvation is best obtained by breaking away from the natural world and from one's sensory and mental experience in it, through asceticism and meditation, in short, by abandoning the body and freeing the soul. In this fashion, saving knowledge that would transform the self would be achieved by way of purification and consequently an ordered way of life. For this reason many retired to the forest and engaged in meditation and dialogue. They were, in effect, "sitting near a teacher." It was the teacher who aided the disciple in the *realization* of the experience of the self's ultimate unity with Brahman, the highest reality. Spiritual inwardness is the main characteristic of the Upanishads. This inwardness aims at the release of the individual from the bonds of egocentric consciousness, of self-enclosed individual existence. In this perspective, the highest reality and ultimate good is to be sought within oneself, for it is the same reality which is the foundation of the objective world. Whereas Kierkegaard and Laing had suggested relatedness—Kierkegaard essentially with God and Laing with others—Hindu thought suggests consciousness of identification with the All. We are reminded here of Narcissus, whose "love for himself is a symbol of longing to escape from the world of conflict and change and to return to a timeless and perfect paradise. . . . The myth symbolizes the attempt to undo ego-segregation,"[7] the attempt at regressive union, and the fatal consequences that can follow upon this misunderstanding of the path. Narcissus might have been rescued by this view of salvation, whose goal is self-transcendence rather than self-absorption.

Along with the conception of reality found in the Upanishads we find the ideas of *karma* and of *transmigration.* Once introduced, these beliefs provided the foundation for all ways of salvation proclaimed in the Indian tradition throughout its history. The human predicament is delineated in the Upanishads as the bondage of the self to the finite conditioned world of appearance. The prescribed remedy—the road to salvation—is the recognition of the unity of the self with the ultimate reality that lies behind appearances. The goal, salvation, is *moksha,* or release from rebirth, which can be achieved only by proper knowledge.

Transmigration is taught in the Brihadaranyaka-Upanishad where it is said that an individual fashions a future existence for himself by his good or bad deeds. The process that is pictured has been going on infinitely. The sphere in which the perpetual births and deaths take place is called Samsara, which is the finite world of appearance. Samsara often is pictured as a wheel because the wheel rolls on endlessly, and often it is depicted as a stream because the water is constantly moving and carrying beings along on its surface. Basically, Samsara is the time-space dimension. It stands for the condition of finitude and separation that we all experience in our lives. It is the life that we are now living and from which in this tradition we want release. Our souls will continue indefinitely on this wheel or stream, taking ever-new forms in life after life until some way of liberation is found. The prospects of living many lives under the conditions of misfortune and suffering filled the ancient sages with dread and they sought earnestly to find a way out of the maze. The links between the doctrines of *karma* and transmigration provided a partial solution.

The doctrine of *karma* explains and provides the justification for the whole process of repeated lives. One's future existence is determined by the law of *karma*—a word that means "deeds" or "works." It is the law that one's thoughts, words, and deeds have ethical consequences, fixing one's lot in future existences (or in one's future). Looked at retrospectively, *karma* is the cause of what is happening in one life now. *Karma* is the cause—one's life is the result or the effect. Simply put, you reap what you sow. Actually, *karma* is a quasi-scientific concept in that it is based on a strict application of the law of cause and effect. Behind this concept is a sense of order in the universe and a strict and clear sense of justice. Ethically speaking then, *karma* means that every good deed brings a corresponding good effect and every bad deed will give rise to an evil result. Generally, the results or effects are considered primarily in relation to the individual self, *not* to society as a whole. A man's deeds shape not only his character but his soul so that in his next incarnation his soul would be reembodied only in a form into which that shape would fit. In the first place, it is possible to emphasize the past, in which case one may develop the attitude of resignation. Basic to resignation is the idea that our present life is merely the result of activity in the past and that there is nothing that can be done about it. Such attitudes enable individuals to accept stoically whatever happens to them. It may also have evil effects, since it can be used to justify the *status quo* by giving present conditions (such as class and race discrimination) an absolute foundation. A more positive aspect is the point emphasized by many modern exponents of Indian philosophy that the concept places man's destiny in his own hands and increases the sense of personal responsibility. It is a concept that also offers hope because a man can better his position in the future through good deeds—that is, through spiritual progress.

The inseparable concepts of *karma* and transmigration expanded the ancient Indian's view of life: he knew that he had passed through innumerable lives from which he might be suffering right now. There was an endless past and an endless future unless he found some way to transcend the system.

The Hindu view of life is a rather discouraging view, yet for the Hindus there is an antidote. If you think that this life is evil and you are distressed by the prospect of endless rebirths, there is a realm of being that is changeless—not at all like this "divided and distinguished" world that is full of change and decay and suffering, into which you can be liberated, if you try. Hindus are saved from pessimism by their belief that this world is not the only realm of existence, that endless suffering and meaninglessness is not their inevitable lot, that all is not hopelessly involved in becoming, changing, disintegrating, and perishing, that there is a realm of *true* being and *true* freedom: Nirvana.

The further history of Indian religions, whether Hindu or Buddhist, is essentially that of the search for the proper solution of the problem: How may one reach a state of being that transcends life's imperfections and dividedness, that is, how can one achieve self-transcendence? This is similar, of course, to the Western concern with how the individual can change his destructive tendency to self-absorption or self-encapsulation. As we have seen, saving knowledge is knowledge that is lived in every thought and action—a transformation of the person himself. True knowledge is true knowledge of Brahman, which is inseparable from an altered way of life.

The method for attaining salvation—*moksha*—is a method of inner purification and meditation. Originally, the path to salvation was by way of sacrificial ritual. In later Indian thought the method proposed for salvation has to do with transformation of consciousness. Yogic exercise and meditation are used to aid the disciple to attain a state of unity with reality, first by subduing the passions and arousing awareness of the inner self. The Upanishads state that this awareness is not attained without fortitude. To see the Self one must become calm, controlled, quiet, patiently enduring and contented. As Kierkegaard said, narrowness is the way. The Upanishads spell out the technique of the realization of identity with or complete absorption into Brahman. In this technique the prospective Brahman knower sits meditating in profound quiet, his mind seeking to know, really know, to be spiritually certain that he

and the world of sense about him have alike the same ground
of being, that he and the tree near him are one, because they
are both phases or aspects of the One.

The certitude of that unity comes to him when he is more
in a nonconscious than a conscious state; strictly speaking, he
would be neither conscious nor unconscious, he would be as in
an ecstasy, which means literally to stand outside oneself or to
be beside oneself.

In seeking analogies for this state, the later Upanishadic
thinkers declared that there are three mental states that may
be compared with it: the state of waking consciousness; the
state of dreaming sleep; and the state of deep dreaming sleep.
As modes of experiencing truth and reality all three states of
consciousness are found to be defective in various degrees. In
the first two, there is a persistence of the consciousness of the
duality of subject and object, self and nonself, ego and nonego
that Hindu thought aims to overcome. Deep dreamless sleep
comes closest to affording an analogy because it represents a
sinking back into a type of nonconsciousness in which subject
and object are no longer distinguished. There is, however, a
fourth state of consciousness that underlies and yet transcends
the first three. It is Pure Consciousness, which comes into full
being only with the experience of union with Brahman. Pure
Consciousness is considered to be the highest of all states of
mind because it represents the purest being of soul when the
soul is sleeplessly intent, when subject and object are indistin-
guishable in the purity of being, in the union of Atman with
Brahman. "The experiencing of this unity with the utmost
intensity was the greatest good ancient oriental religion could
bestow."[8]

The fourth state is not that which is conscious of the subjective nor
that which is conscious of the objective nor that which is conscious
of both, nor that which is simple consciousness, nor that which is an
all-sentient mass, nor that which is all darkness. It is unseen, transcendent, the sole essence of the consciousness of self, the completion of
the world.[9]

This, the final step on the road to salvation, is called the *turiya.* Here, at last, the world and the self are not obliterated, as they would be in deep dreamless sleep, but are instead held together in their pure essence, stripped of all distortion and illusion, united with the being of Brahman-Atman where their reality is found to subsist.

To experience such a state of consciousness is to attain *moksha*—final liberation, release from rebirth. In this, salvation is seen to be attained through superior knowledge or a knowledge that is realization of oneself. Union with Brahman, the ultimate reality that dwells in all things, is considered the highest form of spiritual existence. In this achievement, man comes to see, not his separateness from the gods and his fellows, but his and their identity with an eternal, all-inclusive being or reality. In this mystical union, he finds his deliverance from separateness, from an egocentric consciousness. The Indian sages not only stress that Brahman is the ground of reality, but as the basis of this meditative discipline they stress the fact that the division of the objective and the subjective worlds is erroneous; that the Brahman outside is the same as the Brahman inside oneself. The sage Gargya put this understanding in the form of an aphorism: "The being who is in the mirror— him I meditate upon as Brahman." Note the difference between Narcissus, who saw the reflection of his own *self,* and the Hindu sage, who reflected on the *Self* that is ultimate reality. In other words, the Hindu sage understood that the inner true self is Brahman and that nothing takes place in the individual self that does not have its source and ground in the Self. Brahman, the object of all, and Atman, the inner self, are equated. The ultimate reality is called Brahman-Atman; the objective and subjective are one. Reaching this supreme state is achieved by shutting out the distractions of the external world and turning one's concentration on the interior state. This is an antidote to precisely that narcissism, that egocentrism, which seems to be inherent in the human condition. The viewpoint of Upanishadic philosophy[10] is that we are not simply isolated individuals, like so many pebbles on a beach, but are rather parts of a total reality, and are essentially related to all other beings. In this view, all things can be seen as objects of value and respect because they are all manifestations of the Great Self. In such a view, self-worth is essentially assured.

What is the point of this exposition of Hindu thought—what does it mean? Especially this equation of Atman-Brahman? It means that the Hindu tradition also addresses itself to man's fundamental condition, to his tendency to insecurity and anxiety over his place in the cosmos, over his purpose and worth, and sense of meaninglessness, to his tendency as a consequence to focus on his individual self as a strategy for survival. This tradition says the consciousness that knows the self's identity with the Self is salvation, to lose the self, the false empirical Dharma self in order to gain the inner true Self. East and West, there is agreement that it is the false self that makes the inner true self inaccessible, except by the loss of the old false self to gain the new true being. But whereas the Western tradition says *relationship* is the source of salvation, the Hindu tradition says *identification* with or return to the source is salvation.[11] It has been said that this is narcissism, that in fact mysticism in general is narcissistic. But since the identification with the All can be viewed as identification with Otherness, since Atman, the Self, participates in the essence of Cosmic Reality, it is not self-enclosure. It is not narcissism in the sense in which we have reconsidered and understand it, narcissism as a mode of being that is an attempt to defend against the loss of self—a strategy for survival in dread of nonbeing and unworth, which is inevitably self-defeating. The Hindu view of salvation is in fact the opposite. It is self-transcendence. It is the endeavor to overcome man's sense of abandonment and lovelessness in the cosmos and the egocentric self-centered consciousness that narcissism is by regaining awareness of the connection of the isolated self to the Other. In Hindu thought the world, the objective material world, is defined as a place of suffering and is therefore what we might call a "bad object" against which the individual must defend himself and from which he would like to be released. The Hindu path of salvation offers a release from the suffering of this phenomenal objective world and a way out of narcissistic self-enclosure. Narcissus' attempt to undo separation was not an attempt at reunion with Source or Otherness but rather an immersion in himself, which was fatal.

It could be said that man's religions are an attempt at overcoming man's narcissism, his self-concern, by establishing good "object relations"—to right the relationship that man has a tendency to falsify. In Western Biblical religion, it would be through an I-thou relationship with God and by way of a model of love—Jesus. In the Eastern religions the goal is achieved through harmony with the cosmic order. The goal is a consciousness of being *in* the world, yet not *of* it, for although a transformed consciousness may have achieved the vantage point of a broader level of awareness, the empirical self continues to act in the world. This would be true of the Chinese sage or of a Bodhisattva who forgoes extinction in Nirvana and returns to the world out of love and compassion for its forms. The story of human life thus seems in a sense to be the story of division, isolation, and the recurring story of religions attempting to reassure the individual that he can become whole, that the individual is a part of, not apart from, the whole and can reunite with it or relate to it, that he can "cast away . . . this state of ignorance, be rid of the notion that thou art an outcast in the wilderness."[12] In other words, man can climb over the wall of self-enclosure. Self-transcendence is possible.

Buddhism

The intention of the Buddhist tradition is like that of Hinduism, from which it derived, yet it is also a critique of Hinduism. The goal of Buddhism is to overcome man's predicament, his sorrow, or *dukkha,* which results from the falsification of his relation to reality. Buddhism also addresses itself to man's attachment to self, his preoccupied self-absorption and ego-encapsulation, precisely that narcissism with which we are concerned.

Buddhism, like the other traditions of India and indeed of the West, begins with the experience of sorrow as the inescapable fact and condition of human existence. This "elemental experience of sorrow . . . is the basis on which the higher religious traditions of Eurasia proceed in constructing their salvation programs."[13] The opening passages of Genesis tell of the creation and original paradise, and then of man's separation from this Eden and the entrance of sorrow into human life, which disrupted the entire cosmic order. Ever since this separation took place man has sought a way out either destructively or constructively: destructively by way of self-enclosure, the narcissistic defense, or constructively by seeking a path of salvation that leads to self-transcendence and the restoration of or reunion with the Source.

In the Buddhist view, man's suffering is rooted in a distortion of his perception of the world. Suffering is overcome by knowledge, by enlightenment as to the nature of the self and reality. Buddhists believe that release from sorrow means not only release from the ego but release from the understanding that there is anything but Change. It is an understanding that there is no illusion and no reality, no self and no other, no separation and no attachment. In sum: release from the sorrow of the world involves what appears to be an extreme form of resolving man's predicament. It is the denial not only of the possibility of separation but of the possibility of any attachment. It is the denial of existence of the self in fact, of existence itself. Nirvana is the "blowing out" of existence. "In fact, of the numerous answers that have been offered, during the millenniums, in all quarters of the world, as solutions to life's enigmas, this one must be ranked as the most uncompromising, obscure, and paradoxical."[14]

Our knowledge of Buddhism does not derive from any writings of the Buddha, because he wrote none. With the Buddha, as with many other great teachers, it is striking how much we must depend on the oral tradition, on the spoken word, and on the writings of the disciples. It is from Buddhist monks that we learn how the tradition of the "Awakened One," the Buddha, came into being. The prince Gautama Sakyamuni secretly left his father's kingdom and his own household. This was the second stage of the four stages, or ashramas, in the life plan of one on his way to salvation. The first stage is that of being the student, the second that of the householder, the third that of the hermit or wandering mendicant in the forest, and the fourth that of the Sunnyasin, or holy man. The prince left his father's home in order to become a wandering mendicant and to devote himself to austere practices for those years until he arrived at the threshold of enlightenment. It is said that he spent six years engaged in a profound struggle for the realization of salvation.

According to the legend, the Buddha was particularly anxious not to reject the Brahmin philosophy until he had tested it thoroughly. He spent six years of search among the two widely recognized roads to salvation known to India: philosophic meditation, which stemmed from the tradition of the Vedas and particularly the Upanishads, and the other extreme, the bodily asceticism that stemmed from the tradition of the Hindus called the Jains. The prince gave up his wandering and turned aside at the place now called Bodh Gaya and sat beneath the foot of the fig tree, a tree that came to be known as the knowledge or bodhi tree, or simply the bo tree. There he entered upon a process of meditation that was to affect the thinking of millions of men after him, for Buddhism is the only religious message of India that has spread far beyond its birthplace. While seated beneath the bo tree, Buddha was tempted by the god Kama-Mara (or desire and death), but he overcame the temptation by remaining in meditation and experienced awakening. When he emerged after forty-nine days of meditation, he realized that the experience he had had could not be transmitted. He was prevailed upon by the god Brahma to bring his teachings to the world, to all the deluded beings wrapped in an enclosure of illusion.

The prince then became a teaching Buddha and went back into the world to communicate to others his saving truth—but with reluctance, for the doctrine was meant only for those who were willing to hear. The Buddha, therefore, is known as the silent sage, as Sakyamuni (*sākya*, "his clan"; *muni*, "silent sage"). His teachings offer no theology, no mythological vision, no dogma. Perhaps in Buddhism, more than in any other religion, it is true to say that a diagnosis of the human condition is presented as well as a method of treatment of healing for those interested in following it.

The Buddha's diagnosis of the human predicament is contained in his teaching of what is known as the four noble truths: All life is suffering; the cause of suffering is selfish desire; the way that leads to the end of suffering and desire is the Noble Eightfold Path. The Buddha believed that in the face of despair, one could turn to the law of cause and effect for release from suffering. If the cause could be annihilated, then perhaps its effect could be annihilated. Inquiring into the cause on the psychological level, he found it to lie in ignorant and selfish desire, which is common to all men. It is a function of the ignorance that is inherent in man's existence. We move in a world of illusion and are bound by it, although we think that we know about ultimate reality. As a result, we are caught in a trap, bound by illusion; our ignorance is the cause of the sorrow and the suffering of human life.

The Buddhist's understanding is that our universal condition of malaise is based on our fundamental unawareness, or our unconscious as Freud would have put it. Our unconscious attitudes bind us to the past and determine our future. The Buddhist goes farther than Freud, saying that this inheritance comes from former lives. But the human condition cannot be understood simply in terms of error; it has to be understood in a more ontological fashion as being rooted in the condition of existence itself. The pathological landscape of the soul for the Buddha was the result of cravings of the ego-bound self.

This is a hard diagnosis to accept. We are hardly prepared to believe that we are as unwholesome or unhealthy as that. Pathology is a term used for those few we segregate into asylums. The fate of the myth of Narcissus, our forgetfulness of its tragic end, is itself witness that we have a strong resistance to recognizing our condition. In that resistance lies the tightest knot.

For those who are willing to accept the diagnosis that the Buddha has proposed, however, there is some hope, because he then said that man can be released from suffering. The therapy understood as transformation of one's being prescribed by Buddhist doctrine is the practice of the Noble Eightfold Path: "Now this . . . is the noble truth of the way that leads to the cessation of pain: this is the noble Eightfold Way; namely, right use, right intention, right speech, right action, right lively-hood, right effort, right mindfulness, right concentration."[15] This is the path that leads to the end of desire and the end of sorrow, because it will overcome ignorance and make possible awakening. Here we find not a philosophy but a theory of the technique of liberation from the ego. The Buddhist's prescription is a difficult one.

For those who feel urgently that they would like to undertake the strenuous discipline that the Buddha suggests, and only the hardy will attempt it, his Middle Path is intended. Although the Buddha made the decision to teach his doctrine, it was never meant for any but those who actively wished for it. The Middle Path is the path between two extreme modes of action, not between two doctrines, for Buddhism did not have a metaphysical orientation but was meant to be a way of life offering liberation from the suffering of the human condition. It is aimed at a spiritual goal, the goal of love and peace.

In the sermon in the Deer Park in Benares he said that there are two extremes which are to be avoided. What are the two extremes? A life given to pleasures, which is degrading and profitless. And a life given to mortification or asceticism, which is painful and also profitless. By avoiding these two extremes, the true seeker will follow the Middle Path which leads to insight, to wisdom, to calm, to knowledge, to enlightenment, to Nirvana. The Buddha was marking out a path that would lead to transcendental experience, an experience beyond the enclosure of the ego, or, one might say, an experience of nonego. This requires that the disciple learn the knowledge of nonattachment to worldly existence, the knowledge of repose by way of emancipation from sensations and feelings and thereby release from the bondage of the human condition that causes such suffering.

Although their conclusions differ, both the Buddha and Freud saw the world as projections of one's inner state of unconsciousness or, as Buddha would say, of ignorance. Therefore, the Buddha denied the validity of perceptions and the phenomenal world, whereas Freud claimed that we needed a cleansing of our perceptions in order to see it rightly. Like the existentialists of our own time, the Buddha sensed the transiency of existence. He indicated that the root of human suffering could be found in the attribution of absolute values to what is after all only relative, since it is transient. The world is fundamentally nonsubstantial for the Buddha, having no abiding or permanent essence. Everything is in flux. Existence itself is conditioned by the insight into a reality in which only the law of change is without change. While the initial impact of this awareness of impermanence is despair and the dread of meaninglessness, there is hope in the Buddha's understanding that one could extricate oneself from it in the service of self-transcendence. A cure is indeed possible, if we can be awakened from the dream of ignorance in which our lives pass and follow the Middle Path of Buddha as the spiritual physician.

The steps of the path lead progressively to the perfected disciple, or the *arahat,* and finally to Nirvana, a state in which the disciple knows neither satisfaction nor dissatisfaction and experiences only the consummate purity of poised equanimity. The final goal here is the pure ecstasy (*ekstasis* means "standing outside of oneself") that follows upon the wisdom that releases one from this suffering existence into spiritual realities beyond the capabilities of the self. This expanded or transformed consciousness could be called a cosmic consciousness, an awakening to reality as if life prior to this had been a dreaming sleep, an awakening into Nirvana—which means a "blowing out" of existence. It means having left a state of spiritual ignorance *(avidyā)* and desire *(kāma),* to be awakened to transcendental wisdom *(vidyā)*, which is liberation from the bondage of the self. Vidya is achieved by sacrificing the ego and by self-surrender. This sacrifice of self leads to the Void where one realizes that there has been no path, no world, of the senses, no Samsara, and that there is no Nirvana, since there has never been its opposite. One sees that reality is the state of awakening to the Void in which one is, and yet there is no one to awaken.

Theravada Buddhism is the most extreme doctrine we shall encounter in the attempt to overcome the suffering and separation of life. In the Buddhist transcendence of the ego, one transcends into a reality that is Emptiness. There is no ego and there is no Other. Overcoming self-enclosure, Buddhism leads us into a reality of sheer openness. For the Awakened One there is no enlightenment, only the wisdom of the Void.

Clearly, then, of all the paths suggested to overcome the dread of loneliness, abandonment, and suffering none is so radical as Theravada Buddhism, the original Buddhism of "the Elders." Man's separation and craving for attachment, his clinging to this phenomenal world, his fundamentally dualistic existence, is not overcome by a regaining of attachment to Source, as in other religions, but by release from any attachments whatsoever, from the "cessation of desire"—the "blowing out" of existence, that is, in Nirvana. Buddhism is then not only the overcoming of narcissism but the very extinction of self and world altogether which, according to Buddhist doctrine, is not extinction because there is no such thing as *anything* or *anybody*. Such knowledge, if and when it is realized, effects a transformation of consciousness that releases us from our usual categories of understanding the individual self. Theravada Buddhists believe that all the constituents of existence are anatman, that is, without a self. Anything based on the notion of self is based on a false premise, since according to Buddhist doctrine there is no self that has an independent existence.

The Theravada Buddhist path of recovery from suffering is personal and pragmatic. Salvation, liberation, is an individual problem. A person starts where he is and works toward enlightenment by his own efforts, knowing only that existence is characterized by *dukkha* and that that is rooted in ignorance. The way out of this state is through an elimination of "selfish desire," via the Buddha's Noble Eightfold Path which will lead those who are able to follow it to Nirvana.

In the Mahayana doctrine—the "great vehicle" of salvation, Buddhism as it developed and spread through the Northern Asian countries after the death of Buddha—the early rigorous philosophy of the original Buddhism is transformed into an optimistic religion. The Bodhisattva, one whose essence *(sattva)* is enlightenment *(bodhi),* is endowed with the power to save the individual, who does not have to struggle on his own for salvation. The Bodhisattva of Mahayana Buddhism is one who has attained Nirvana but has returned to the world out of love and compassion for its forms. The discipline that the Buddhist must undergo to become a Bodhisattva creates tremendous stores of energy that might be expressed as tyrannically repressed feelings and desire. Unless the Bodhisattva is truly without any ego, he could be subject to the sort of temptation that would suddenly cause him to release this store of energy in a destructive direction. On the contrary nothing can touch his self-sufficiency, but it is a self-sufficiency that requires a continuous nonexperience of ego.

Even so brief an outline suggests that the Buddhist tradition evolved from an impersonal and rigorous discipline to which an individual subjected himself on the path to Nirvana into a religion based on love and compassion, the personal saving grace of the Bodhisattva. In Mahayana Buddhism the essence or Suchness of the Universe is identified with the sort of love behind things that produces Buddhas—it is a Buddha essence at the heart of the Universe. In this, the Buddhas as expressions or projections of being itself are not merely indifferent or unfeeling expressions of it, but rather a manifestation of a compassionate essence. Thus, in Mahayana Buddhism it is redemptive love that draws ignorant, clouded minds along the Bodhisattva way of life back to itself, whereas the ideal of

Theravada Buddhism is the Arahat: the self-perfected disciple whose salvation is entirely an individual matter. In Mahayana, on the other hand, salvation is gained together with others not merely for the sake of oneself alone but to open the possibility of Buddhahood to everyone.

Some aspects of Mahayana Buddhist teachings indicate their attempt to overcome the fundamental problem of the ego-bound self. Here, too, in the ideal of the Bodhisattva, we find Mahayana Buddhism's attempt to overcome man's tendency to reflect the image and the figure of Narcissus as the metaphor of man's condition. As we have seen, the test of the Bodhisattva is his readiness to give boundlessly. This requires a constant abdication or nonexperience of ego. The whole sense of Bodhisattvahood is that the limited and circumscribing ego has vanished and that in the Perfection of Wisdom the Bodhisattva knows the nonexistence of all phenomenal values on the transcendental plane. By eliminating all "selfish desires," by not craving for anything at all, he transcends himself as an individual and, in so doing, becomes established in a spiritual sphere of force and energy that is available for the benefit of those who ask him. The discipline is now directed not toward the individual for his own sake but toward the universal for the sake of others. It is a *selfless* state. The Bodhisattva remains *in* this world, not *of* it. The Bodhisattva is constantly self-transcending, until he actually lives instinctively without his ego and its illusions. This transformation is the perfection of wisdom in which the pathological landscape of the soul—the pathology of self-encapsulation—is healed.

It is important to remember that the aim of Buddhism is not to deny commonsense reality as experienced in the commonsense world, but to cleanse one's vision of false views, and so to be able to receive the world "as it really is," that is, to see its "suchness" *(tathatā)*.

Buddhism in China is called Ch'an and in Japan, Zen. The word comes from the Sanskrit word *dhyāna,* meaning "meditation." In Zen, as in the highly descriptive image of St. John of the Cross, man may be compared to a window through which the light of God is shining. If the windowpane is clear, then the pane is completely transparent and we do not see it at all. It is "empty" and nothing is seen but the light shining through. If, however, a man "bears in himself the stains of spiritual egotism and preoccupation with his illusory and exterior self then the window pane itself is clearly seen by reasons of the stains that are on it."[16] And so it was with the self-encapsulated Narcissus, looking into the pool of water and seeing only his own reflection. The Zen Buddhist doctrine of "emptiness" "corresponds . . . psychologically to selflessness or Innocence, when *'Avidya'* (ignorance) and *bodhi* (enlightenment) are one." It is the self cleansed of the "pollution [that] comes from the egocentric consciousness which is Ignorance."[17] Emptiness signifies the self's transparence and is the corollary of Kierkegaard's "purity of heart" which "wills one thing." Emptiness—the innocence of the self—is not sheer passivity but rather the effortless "no striving" activity of the self "when it is restored to wholeness." This *restitutio ad integram* is the goal of Zen training—which pushes contradictions to "their ultimate limit where one has to choose between madness and innocence."[18]

The doctrine of Zen Buddhism makes it quite clear that the pathology of man is the pathology of Narcissus. Self-centeredness, self-preoccupation, is at the root of the problem. Both Hinduism and Buddhism recognize this pathology and also recognize that this is a destructive gesture toward life and is not true being but is rather a response to the predicament in which man finds himself and which he must transcend if he is to be healed. Self-enclosure seems to be a universally recognized form of madness whether we view it in the light of the myth or from the point of view of Kierkegaard's understanding or Laing's, the Hindu's or the Buddhist's. We seem to have to choose between faith and sin as Kierkegaard said, sanity and madness as Laing put it, or, as in Buddhism, between innocence and madness.

The Zen Buddhist tradition, like the Christian tradition, involves a therapeutic course. To understand these therapeutic methods, one can broadly discriminate between two kinds of wisdom: the wisdom of words and statements, a rational, dialectical kind of wisdom, and a different sort of wisdom that goes beyond the reach of reason, which is paradoxical and experiential. For transformation to take place one must get down underneath the wisdom of speech to a language that at first seems baffling. As Kierkegaard said he had to wound from behind, so Zen Buddhists use the language of the seemingly illogical and the paradoxical, the koan. In Zen, the communication intended is not a message that *informs,* but an experience that *transforms* consciousness.

> A monk asks Pai-Chang,
>   "Who is the Buddha?"
> Pai-Chang answers:
>   "Who are you?"

The koan (or *Kung-an* in Chinese) is a puzzle or problem that is within us to which the Zen master points so that it can be brought out of the unconscious into the field of consciousness. The purpose of koans is to affect awakenings. They sound impossible, even nonsensical, but they cannot and are not intended to be understood on the plane of logic or intellection. It is believed that the very nonsensicality of a koan can shock us into penetrating the veil that clouds our vision. The Zen masters were concerned to discover an effective means leading to the Zen experience. They were not interested in questions that require intellectual answers, they wanted the disciples to find the answers. "For Zen . . . there must be a certain awakening which breaks up the equilibrium and brings one back to the . . . borderline between the conscious level and the unconscious. Once this level is touched, one's ordinary consciousness becomes infused with the unconscious."[19] Initially, then, it seems that the individual in this discipline is in a state of uniformity or what, in a modern analysis, is similiar to a narcissistic transference in which no distinction is made between I and Other, but then the Zen disciple is pushed into the corner and asked to make a complete about-face so that he can "wake up." This will break up the equilibrium, and the recognition will occur of his essential relatedness to his Source or, as D. T. Suzuki puts it, "This is the moment when the finite mind realizes that it is rooted in the infinite."[20]

The language used by Zen is deliberately a radical reversal of the usual logic of language because the dilemma of human communication is that although we need to use words, our experience tends to be falsified by that very verbalization. Zen, therefore, tries to use language that makes us awaken directly to experience. Zen rejects systematic elaboration in order to go to direct experience, to the realization of the Buddha, of the unity of the phenomenal, visible world with the noumenal, invisible world, the realization that division, separation, is untruth. As Suzuki said:

The Zen approach is to enter right into the object itself and see it, as it were, from the inside. To know the flower is to become the flower, to be the flower, to bloom as the flower. . . . When this is done, the flower speaks to me and I know all its secrets. . . . Not only that: along with my "knowledge" of the flower I know all the secrets of the universe, which includes all the secrets of my own Self, which has been eluding my pursuit all my life so far, because I divided myself into a duality.[21]

The realization of unity is perfect mirror knowledge:

The mirror is thoroughly egoless and mindless. If a flower comes it reflects a flower, if a bird comes it reflects a bird. . . . Everything is revealed as it is. There is no discriminating mind or self-consciousness on the part of the mirror. If something comes, the mirror reflects; if it disappears the mirror just lets it disappear . . . no traces of anything are left behind. Such non-attachment, the state of no-mind, or the truly free-working of a mirror is compared here to the pure and lucid wisdom of Buddha.[22]

This is the consciousness that lies underneath and beyond cultural structures and forms and intellectual concepts.

The goal of Zen training, then, is to overcome "egocentric interest," which is the concomitant of duality, so that "a life of freedom and spontaneity [can be realized] where such disturbing feelings as fear, anxiety, or insecurity"[23] cannot assail man. It is this anxiety and insecurity to which we want to address ourselves because it is my contention that it is out of anxiety that the egocentric interests arise and not the other way around. We have seen that Kierkegaard and Laing understood this, as do many modern psychoanalysts. In Zen, to know "thyself" is to know thy Self. As Suzuki has pointed out, "Everything without tells the individual that he is nothing, while everything within persuades him that he is everything."[24] Zen would have man look within and "he will then realize that he is not lonely, forlorn, and deserted; there is within him a certain feeling of a royally magnificent aloneness, standing all by himself and yet not separated from the rest of existence. This unique situation . . . is brought about when he approaches reality in the Zen way."[25] However, when the self attempts to *make* itself unique and becomes extremely self-conscious in its attempt to appear other than itself, one loses one's self actually and then

the real Self is pushed back and is frequently reduced to a nonentity, which means that it is suppressed. And we all know what this suppression means. For the creative unconscious can never be suppressed; it will assert itself in one way or another. When it cannot assert itself in the way natural to it, it will break all the barriers, in some cases violently and in others pathologically. In either way the real Self is hopelessly ruined.[26]

This is precisely what we have heard from everyone and it is to this in fact that all religious disciplines address themselves. Suzuki says: "Worrying over this fact, Buddha declared the doctrine of annatta . . . or non-ego to wake us from the dream of appearances. . . . The real Self is a kind of metaphysical self in opposition to the psychological or ethical self which belongs to the finite world of relativity."[27] It is then the metaphysical self that can transcend itself, while it is the psychological self that is ego-bound.

When the finite self realizes that it is rooted in the infinite, the transcendent, the disciple comes upon what is known in

Buddhism as "mirror knowledge," when "the darkness of the unconscious is broken through and one sees all things as one sees one's face in the brightly shining mirror."[28] This is not the mirror of Narcissus, which reflects only his own ego-encapsulated self, but the mirror that reflects an undistorted reality.

Confucianism

So far, we have concentrated on the religions stemming from the Hindu tradition, the Theravada Buddhism that developed in India and its development into Mahayana Buddhism, which spread into China and combined with Taoist influence to evolve into Ch'an Buddhism or Zen in Japan. But even so brief a review of Eastern thought about man's relations to existence must include two major Eastern traditions that have reflected the self-understanding of millions of people for almost three thousand years: Confucianism and Taoism. In these traditions, too, we find the human situation diagnosed and faced in a similar fashion and there, too, we find the image of Narcissus.

The problem for man in Confucius' time, as in every age, was: How can men live together without destroying one another? Again we find the question of destructiveness and violence in human history and the absence of love. When old ideals and traditions break down—a problem we are aware of today—what is to provide life with a sense of meaning and to hold the social order together? One of the important manifestations of this difficult social situation in Confucius' day was the growing individualism that resulted from the disappearance of the feudal order. Communal thought, which submerged the individual to the interest of the whole, had given way to selfish and personal considerations. Mere appeal to ancestors and traditions could no longer assure that proper social actions would be taken. The Confucian response was to aim at a harmony between man and the moral order. In Confucian thought the moral order took the place of the cosmic order in Hindu thinking in which the individual aimed to achieve tranquillity through union. This was achieved in Buddhist thought through detachment from the world. Self-transcendence was to be achieved by a harmonious relationship between the individual and the moral order. The root of the problem was seen in selfish desires, in egocentricity. Confucianism proposed that selfish individualism be overcome and the common good be secured through the attainment of five cardinal virtues, symbolized by a flowering fruit tree:

jen   moral perfection (the root)
yi   righteousness by justice (the trunk)
li   religious and moral ways of acting (the branches)
ch'ih   wisdom (the flower)
hsin   faithfulness (the fruit)

These basic virtues were concepts expressing the Confucian ideal of the good life: the harmonious well-being of the individual and the community ideally resembled the perfect unity of the tree. *Li,* which is one of the central words in Confucian thought, is difficult to translate, since it means different things in different contexts. The usual, although not always adequate translation, is "propriety." It means the moral way of life and, in the historical-social context, it means an ideal social order. It can also be defined as the way things *ought* to be done. *Li,* then, is the very foundation of the social order but it is not merely a human structure, for it has the sanction of heaven. "Li, said Confucius, is the principle by which the ancient kings embodied the laws of Heaven and regulated the expressions of human nature. Therefore, he who has attained Li, lives, and he who has lost it, dies. . . . Li is based on Heaven, patterned on Earth. . . . Therefore, the Sage shows the people this principle of a rationalized social order and through it everything becomes right in the family, the state, and the world."[29] The ideograph with which *li* is written is composed of two parts, one indicating communication with the supernatural and a second element, originally a pictograph of a sacrificial vessel containing some object. This makes quite explicit the religious bases for proper social behavior and, as Confucius said, "What

I learned is this, that of all things that people live by, Li is the greatest." By the practice of *li*, the principal relationships in society can be so regulated and made right that complete harmony may reign in each home, village, and throughout the empire, ultimately creating a cosmic harmony between men, earth, and heaven and thus put into action among men the Tao, or will of heaven. Confucius' own words:

If there be righteousness in the heart, there will be beauty in the character.
If there be beauty in the character, there will be harmony in the home.
If there be harmony in the home, there will be order in the nation.
If there be order in the nation, there will be peace in the world.[30]

The "root" of the Confucian tree means the will to seek the good of others. Thus, the Confucian mode of overcoming the encapsulated ego was by stressing proper human relationships. The Chinese character for *jen* is a composite of two characters, one for man and the other for two. It stands, therefore, for a man's inclusion of a second person in his plans. It expresses moral perfection and means human-heartedness. This mode of self-discipline is clearly quite different from the meditative disciplines of Hinduism or the practices of Buddhism, but all share the goal of dealing with man's egocentricity and self-encapsulation. Confucianism is unique in its stress on moral relationships—on the harmony in the social order that is the proper goal for man. That goal is to be achieved through the proper attitudes in the fundamental human relationships. The five great pairs of relationships are:

Kindness in the father, filial piety in the son
Gentility in the eldest brother, humility and respect in the younger
Righteous behavior in the husband, obedience in the wife
Humane consideration in elders, deference in juniors
Benevolence in rulers, loyalty in ministers and subjects

If these ten attitudes, the ten *yi*, are generally present in society, then the highest propriety, *li*, will be actualized and harmony will reign between individuals. These attitudes indicate what it is to be truly a man and how one must be in various relationships with other men. In these attitudes people will show their real human character, that is, *jen*. Then there will be happiness among friends, harmony in the home, and peace in the state. The process of Confucian thought moves from the individual to the family to the nation to the world. In the life of the individual and the family, Confucius provided the paradigm for understanding and regulating the larger social and political life. The foundation of civilization according to Confucius rests upon the individual and what he values in life.

Now the ideal man, on whom Confucius believed the foundation of civilization rested, on whom the moral order rested, and on whom harmonious relationship rested, was the superior man, the Chun-tzu. The harmony he sought could not issue from the superficial observance of rules and ceremonies but from a basic feeling of mutuality with others. His inner motives had to match his exterior conduct; there had to be integrity in his good will. There was no understanding in Confucian thought of an inherent depravity in man or a wrongness in the human condition. For Confucius, as for Socrates, to know the good is to do it. Therefore education was stressed to improve the inherently good human nature and to undo the self-centeredness and selfishness that man has a tendency to develop. According to Confucius, the individual human being has dignity by virtue of participation in *li*, participation in the ordered relationships of the community. When he speaks of what it is to be a man he speaks not of the self's cultivation of itself, but a man whose significance lies in his participation in the moral order. To establish human relationships, relationships defined by tradition, which if properly respected assure harmony with the moral order is the Confucian goal for man. Transformation in Confucian understanding is achieved, as we said, not by meditation or other practices but by ritual participation which is communal, a part of the social order, for a man must include another in his plans and according to the appropriate relationship. According to Confucius, "Virtue does not exist in isolation; there must be neighbors."[31] Clearly, its emphasis on human relationships, on including another man in one's plans, on participation in communal ritual, Confucian thought addresses itself to man's tendency to be self-centered and egotistic. The principle of *li*, in particular, indicates a clear understanding of the sacred context of human relationships by virtue of which man participates in the sacral order and transcends himself by being in harmony with the cosmic moral order. For Confucius the Tao, the Way, was a moral way shaped by *li* and in this, as in the other paths of liberation we have looked at, there is no place for self-centeredness, for pride, for a self-enclosed ego. The individual is on the Path or he is lost.

We find in neo-Confucian thought an insistence that "self-transcendence should be attained not by denying one's humanity but by affirming it, by overcoming selfishness in daily life, identifying with others, and coming to an awareness of man's ethical and cultural activity as participating in the creative process of Heaven-and-earth."[32] This doctrine was emphasized especially in contrast to the Buddhist identification of life with suffering and illusion and its insistence "that man could discover his true identity only by negating and *then* transcending his ordinary humanity, that is, recognizing it as an unreal distinction in an illusory world."[33] Confucian thought, on the other hand, is "both this worldly and other worldly."[34]

What is it that makes man go astray in Confucian understanding? To some extent it is fate, or *ming*, but essentially what causes man to go astray in this view is the effect of external objects that lead man to abandon his capacity to have an "evaluating mind." A man must then learn to master things and regain his natural tranquillity, the tranquillity he had at birth, which a man has when he is not involved in externals. It is clear that "environmental conditions, for the ancient Chinese, were the primary source of evil. . . . Evil could not be traced to the inherent nature of any man. The social consequence of external interference, which prevents men from guiding their conduct according to the dictates of their evaluating minds, is that selfish interests (szu) prevail over the interests of society as a whole. Men try to satisfy their own needs and interests or those of their families and care little about the plight of others."[35] There is always a right inclination that the discriminating or evaluating mind must distinguish or he will be led astray by a tendency that is not in accord with *li*. Here again we find that the diagnosis of the human predicament lies in man's self-awareness. The goal in Confucian thought is to regain the Way by a rigorous discipline of learning to live in accord with *li*. For "the more one models oneself on another, the more one loses one's own ego." The ideal is selflessness. In this view, the cultivation of the self meant learning to overcome the distractions of the external world through one's own efforts; with the help of teachers and the guidance of models the student learns to use his inherent and innate qualities and mind to conduct himself in a proper fashion. In this manner he learns to follow the Way.

This is not merely a superficial conformance to rules but rather a self-cultivation so strenuous that eventually the discipline fundamental to the "evaluating mind" would so transform the Confucian sage that he would effortlessly select the right course of action because regulation of a man's conduct by *li* trained the inner man so that his actions are quite natural and spontaneous. "The sage gives reign to his desires and satisfies his passions; nevertheless he is controlled by principle, so why need he be forced or repressed or anxious? For the acting out of the right Way (Tao) by the benevolent (jen) man is without effort."[36] He would be so well disciplined that the external world would not lead him astray. He could respond with equilibrium to the situation in which he finds himself, and the environmental conditions that are understood as a source of evil would no longer have control over him nor be able to make him anxious. He would in this respect have achieved tranquillity. He would no longer fear harm from others, for he would be a man of *jen,* of human-heartedness, in which he would find contentment and which would in turn make other men tranquil. Having achieved tranquillity, he will have been restored to his true nature, his original state before the aberrant condition of man set in. His condition would be one of harmony with the Tao. The "noble man is the man who most perfectly having given up self, ego, obstinacy and personal pride (9:4) follows not profit, but the Way."[37] Thus, Confucianism, despite its seeming emphasis on the this-worldly, is "world transcending."[38] It sees the way out of the disorder and destructiveness of the human predicament as the achievement of harmony among men, based on their harmony with a larger order beyond the self, the moral order of the cosmos—that is, by way of self-transcendence. Here again *self*-transcendence is the antidote to Narcissus.

Taoism

If separation from the Way is understood as being out of the order of *li,* in untranquil disharmony with the *moral* order of the cosmos for the Confucian, so separation from the Way as the *natural* order meant disharmony and a resultant untranquillity for the Taoist. Both Confucianism and Taoism, the two most influential indigenous doctrines of China, shared the cosmic principle of the Tao as a way of accounting for the evident order of the universe. It is not the exclusive property of the Taoists, for it is, in fact, central to the Chinese world view. The harmony manifest in heaven and earth is, in this perspective, the result of the cosmic energy of the Tao—the "path" or "way to go." Taoism, however, provides a somewhat different perspective, since it stresses the development of the inner self in relationship to nature, whereas Confucius stressed the observable behavior of the self in relation to other human beings and the social order. In Taoism social values and social existence appear to be denied. However, this dichotomy is not entirely true and is noted in order to clarify the basic difference in the ways of thought. The Confucian and Taoist views cannot be taken as entirely contrary, because ultimately both agree that ideal existence depends on the character of the individual. The Confucian nobleman, the Chun-tzu, becomes so well trained and disciplined that he acts spontaneously. The goal of the Taoist also is spontaneous action, although it is not dependent on those methods of training. The difference between the two ways lies mainly in their methods for developing the ideal traits of character. In fact, they might be considered complementary aspects of the Chinese character. Confucius believed in imitating the modes and models of the past. Taoism, on the other hand, looked upon nature rather than tradition or culture as a model of the ideal life. Where Confucius stressed the educable nature of man and the virtue or power of discipline based on *li,* Taoism regards man as an aspect of nature, a part of the natural world, whose problems are the result of disharmony with nature. As a part of nature, man is innately good according to the Taoist and his nature needs only to be allowed to express itself naturally and spontaneously. In order to bring out the true nature of man, one must identify himself with the life of nature surrounding him. This involves a way of life that in most interpretations means a withdrawal from society in order to draw closer to nature.

It must be stressed that in both Taoism and Confucianism, as distinct from any of the other systems considered, man's nature is regarded as essentially good, and the values by which he is to live should arise, ideally, spontaneously from within his own nature. However, both admit, he has a tendency to go astray—to leave the Way—which the Confucians believe can be converted by education, the Taoists by conforming with nature.

Before it is possible to understand clearly or to talk about the Taoist understanding of the human condition, however, we must ask, What is Tao? As we know from the opening of the *Tao Te Ching* (Book of the Way and Its Power), the aphoristic writings of Taoism attributed to Lao Tzu, "the Tao that can be told is not the true Tao." The Tao that *can* be told refers to the Confucian code of the social norms and virtues and the carefully defined human relationships—to the "rectification of names." It has to do with discrimination, the discriminating mind which evaluated qualities of good and bad, right and wrong, noble and base. In contrast to the Tao that can be told, Lao Tzu and Chuang Tzu, his disciple, used the term "Tao" to refer to the essentially nameless, to that which is without distinctions to a unitary principle or force underlying the natural order that is responsible for its forms and changes. It is the nameless, the nothingness or nonbeing, that is the Tao from which everything has risen.

Tao is both source and source of direction. This principle was part of the Chinese world view prior to the formation of Taoism or Confucianism. Both schools of thought used the term. Originally Tao probably was used to refer to various aspects of the regularity of nature that ancient people could observe—the alternation of night and day, the seasons, the waxing and waning of the moon, and so on. Thus, Tao, the way, was the path that nature traveled. It was the way of the cosmos, which worked with a wonderful perfection and harmony because the Tao that is the eternal way of the universe is not hindered in its smooth operation. Nevertheless, the Tao ultimately is inexpressible, inconceivable, and nameless. It is wrapped in cosmic mystery and yet all that there is has emerged from its unactualized essence, its unrealized potentiality, or nonbeing. It is the sole source of the act of power or the *te* in all existing things. As with Brahman in Hinduism and the Void in Mahayana Buddhism, it is hard to characterize this ultimate reality. Although the Tao in itself is unknowable, man must not stop in his quest to come to an understanding of it. It is dynamic in its own silent and quiet way. Therefore it can be known through its active power, its *te*, which is a complementary concept in relation to the Tao. Everything that exists has its *te*, its potentiality. *Te* is the operation of the Tao in all existing things; it is, then, through the observation of the dynamics or the *te* in nature that man can apprehend Tao.

The inquiries of the Taoist led then into the realm of nonbeing, or potentiality, to ask how the Tao operates in the realm of actuality or being. The central question of the *Tao Te Ching* considers that *the chief aim of human existence* must be to attain fullness of life by harmony with the Tao. The centrality and the importance of this issue can be easily seen, for just as the natural order functions in perfection and harmony if the Tao is allowed to take its course, unhindered, so man can attain well-being only by conformity and harmony with the Tao. However, man has the power to choose his own way and to make his own plan for himself and his life. In Taoism, it is understood that man has the freedom to go astray, in fact *a tendency* to go astray. As in Confucianism, not conforming to *li* is what leads man to stray. However, the natural order (unlike *li*) is undiscriminating. Ethical distinctions between good and bad are not made. It is from man's tendency to divide himself from his Source in the Tao, from not being in harmony with it, that have sprung all the ills and pains of man and the predicament in which he finds himself. He has chosen in an ego-bound fashion to move contrary to the eternal Tao. In a sense, man has been swimming against the current, for nature is fighting him by flowing the other way. By defying his nature, man finds himself in a troubled condition. The goal of Taoism then (if Taoism can be said to be goal-oriented) would be for man to stop in this contrary movement to the Tao and to become harmonious with it. People who do not follow the Tao may meet with worldly or temporary success, but ultimately their worldly path has "to return" or "revert," for according to Lao Tzu, "Returning is the motion of the Tao."[39] The *Tao Te Ching* tells us that if you "stretch a bow to the full, you will wish you had stopped in time; temper a sword to its sharpest, and you will find it soon grows dull."[40] The process of reversion and return is universal and all natural process is marked by it: coming into being, reaching maturity, and reverting to nonbeing or death. All things go back to their common origin; ultimately they all blend into one.

The wise man knows that he is himself one with all things. Therefore he yields himself to the Tao and neither struggles to assert himself aggressively, nor strives for a sharply distinguishable being of his own. The acceptance of the Tao is quite different from the Buddhist despair that says, "Leave this world of suffering," although in both instances the intention is to transcend the ego. In all the great traditions, it is harmony with the Source and self-transcendence that is sought, while division from the Source—self-encapsulation—and disharmony with it are understood to be the ground of the predicament of man. It is this separation which causes disharmony in the cosmos and disharmony in man himself, separation from Source and self-enclosure not only create disharmony in the cosmic order but are destructive of Being and the well-being of man. The egoic encapsulated mode of existence is self-destructive, as we learned from Narcissus. In accord with this understanding of the Tao as ultimate reality and the unitary principle or source of all that there is, the sage seeks union with the Tao as the first condition of his own well-being. The Taoist sage understood that all things are equally of value: "The special qualities man has are temporary, and thus are insignificant. The whole intent is to end thought about man's uniqueness, to drive man from the center of the stage."[41] Man's tendency to self-centeredness and the intention to overcome that tendency is central in Taoist thought which understands it as inimicable to man's well-being and to the well-being of the natural order. For man to be tranquil (rather than anxious, self-preoccupied, and self-concerned) was the goal of Taoism.

The man of perfect virtue in Taoist thought—and the Taoists held that the object of life should be the cultivation of inner power or virtue—is described as one in whom all actions issue forth spontaneously and without premeditation. Taoists were critical of Confucian emphasis on rites because for them it seemed mere artificiality that hindered man's true nature from emerging. Consequently, Taoists criticize the conscious cultivation of the self or modeling oneself on the image of the Tao, although paradoxically this is what they recommend in order for them to act spontaneously. Of course, there is also a deep human truth involved in this paradoxical view of the Taoist, for it reflects Paul's understanding that the good we would do, we do not, and that which we would not, we do. In other words, our conscious intentions and our unconscious intentions often do not coincide. If we have to make a conscious effort to do good, are we not having to make that effort because of our fundamental desire or inclination not to do good?

The central consideration of the *Tao Te Ching* as to how a man must conduct himself in order to regain his natural harmony with the universe may be stated positively and negatively. Positively stated, the therapeutic principle is that one must exhibit within oneself and reflect the process of the Tao and be characterized by its quiet attitude of power, its production without possession, its action without self-assertion, and development without domination. Negatively stated, the principle is as follows: man must not interfere with the smooth course of Nature going on her way. It is wise to trust the wisdom of the Tao, to waiver practice, which refers to the absence of purposeful activity, to noninterference, reflecting, and not acting in conflict with the Tao which simply unfolds. It is a disinterested, nonmeddlesome, nonaggressive kind of action. As the *Tao Te Ching* puts it, "The sage carries on his business without action, and gives his teachings without words."[42] This nonpurposive activity also implies a disinterestedness in respect to evaluating and making distinctions in contrast to the Confucian view of the need to understand and define the relationships of the social order—the "rectification of names"—on which harmony rests. The mind of the Taoist sage, in the belief that the Tao is "nameless," should neither discriminate nor evaluate but should be a mirror, much as Freud said the analyst should be in respect to his analysand. Everything in the universe is acceptable as a natural process, even death. The restoration that occurs in the Taoist sage reunites him with his Source in a "Return" movement to a unity with the undifferentiated source, the state of dreaming innocence of the infancy of man and of man's unfancy. At this point the sage would have achieved tranquillity and the union between the self and the other, the Tao within and the Tao without.

The sage puts his own person last and it comes first, treats it as extraneous to himself and is preserved. Is it not because he is without thought of self that he is able to accomplish his private aims?[43]

The goal and spirit of Chinese thought, as Fung Yu-lan has said, was to make clear what is the "highest form of achievement of which a man *as* a man is capable. According to the Chinese philosophers, it is nothing less than being a sage, and the highest achievement of a sage is the identification of the individual with the universe."[44]

In order to achieve this, he "makes the Tao the door."[45] The Taoist sage would not only adapt to things as they are, but the ideal Taoist simply left things alone. This "laissez-faire" attitude, the doctrine of nonactivity, or *wu wei,* suggests that things should be allowed to develop according to their own natures. In this view, man's problems begin when he acts on the basis of artificiality and arbitrariness—the self-consciousness and deliberateness of the state of knowledge—rather than in harmony with the Tao. The Taoist approach of *wu wei* does offer a spiritual truth on the conduct of life, which like the other disciplines we have discussed reminds us that self-centeredness and egocentricity are characteristic of our central predicament, to gain ourselves is to "let go" of self and its ambitions and desires. We have found this at the root of all the major religious traditions. It is the central problem to which they address themselves. Eastern thought instructs us that Narcissus reflects the universal human condition, not only that of man in Western culture. It tells us that the root of man's predicament is, like that of Narcissus, one of inordinate self-concern and egocentricity. The liberation given from this inevitably troubled, anxious, and self-destructive condition is the goal of their teachings, and the way, always difficult, is by regaining a harmonious relationship to man's source—to otherness. In other words, by self-transcendence. Everywhere we find that separation means death, and that attachment, or union, means life. Narcissus' other name is death.

It is precisely to this problem that modern psychoanalytic

thought addresses itself. It attempts to understand how it is that man has a universal tendency to "go astray," to be self-absorbed—narcissistic—and to understand the fatality of this course. It is to that body of thought we now turn.

6
Narcissism Reconsidered:
The Psychoanalytic Approach

> Psychoanalysis appears to be more than merely one among many possible theories about the psyche; rather it comes close to being the systematic consciousness that a certain epoch has of the nature and character of its soul.
>
> *Erich Heller*[1]

> Are we all in fact
>   unloving and unlovable?
> Then one *is* alone. . . .
>
> *T. S. Eliot*[2]

WE TURN to psychoanalytic thought for several reasons. For one, psychoanalysis has in common with the religious paths of liberation the goal of transforming the individual's consciousness, of releasing him from his self-centered, egocentric, isolated consciousness into *"the optimum* knowledge of truth, and that is knowledge of reality."[3] For another, as Foucault tells us, "Psychoanalysis . . . form[s] an undoubted and inexhaustible treasure-hoard of experiences and concepts, and above all a perpetual principle of dissatisfaction, of calling into question . . . of what may seem in other respects to be established."[4] There is yet a third reason. Concerning the theological significance of psychoanalysis, Paul Tillich wrote that therapeutic psychology represents a rediscovery of the spiritual heritage of the West that has been forgotten. It represents "a rediscovery of the meaning of the word 'sin' [as] universal tragic estrangement . . . from one's essential being. . . . Depth psychology has helped theology to rediscover the demonic structures that determine our consciousness and our decisions. . . . And it is indeed important to know that theology had to learn from the psychoanalytic method the meaning of grace, the meaning of

128

forgiveness as acceptance."[5] Lastly and most importantly, we turn to psychoanalysis because it has been concerned, increasingly in recent years, with man's "pride," his tendency to egocentricity and its destructiveness—with narcissism.

Sigmund Freud considered the narcissistic disorders manifesting reversion of the libido, withdrawal, self-absorption, and megalomania, inaccessible to treatment. To him they presented a stone wall, since narcissistic patients seemed incapable of transference. Without the ability to link significant persons in one's early life with the analyst, the therapeutic process is unable to work through the resistance. Resistance was understood by Freud to be the obstacle to making the unconscious conscious. Freud's earliest statements on the subject indicated that he understood narcissism to be significant not simply as a perversion in which the subject takes himself as an object of love but significant as a universal phenomenon of human development. He indicated that a "disposition of the libido [psychosexual energy] which must be described as narcissistic might have to be reckoned with in a much wider field [than has been thought] and that it might claim a place in the regular sexual development of human beings."[6] As such it would be a universal aspect of the development of the individual, the "reservoir" and "universal original condition out of which *object-love* develops later."[7] The term "object" in the context of this chapter refers to "other" and "not-self." He describes a narcissistic disposition of the libido as one that displays the characteristics of megalomania and as being *withdrawn* from interest in the world of people and things. In the narcissistic disorders the "main characteristic . . . is that . . . *the investment of objects with libido is lacking.*" In other words, the narcissistic individual is turned away from the world around him. When Freud raised the question of what has happened to the energy diverted from the "objects" of the world, he suggested as an answer that this energy "is turned back upon the ego—the narcissistic individual is self-*absorbed,* self-centered and that *this reflex reversion of it is the source of the delusions of grandeur.*" In Freud's terms, "the name for this utilization of the libido [is] Narcissism." At this point what we have is only the half-image of Narcissus as the self-loving man. That there is such a reciprocity of libido between ego and objects that it can be directed outward or retracted into the self is, according to Freud, the only explanation that helps to solve the "riddle of the narcissistic neuroses." This process, the transformation of object libido into ego libido, as for instance in sleep, in itself is not pathogenic. Freud went on to explain, however, that "it is quite a different matter when a definite, very forcible process compels the withdrawal of the libido from its objects." What that compelling force may be, Freud did not suggest, although he made it clear that it is not *simply* self-love. But with this suggestion, various threads begin to be woven into the fabric of what we call narcissism: "The libido that has then become narcissistic can no longer find its way back to its objects." The consequent "damming up of the libido in the ego becomes pathogenic."[8]

Freud concluded that "megalomania then represents the mastery of this volume of libido."[9] This megalomania may result when the ego, having directed its libido outward originally to avoid falling ill of its excess, is thwarted. In "the last resort, we must begin to love in order that we may not fall ill, and must fall ill if, in consequence of frustration we cannot love."[10] Freud suggests, by way of analogy, that "a person suffering organic pain and discomfort relinquishes his interest in the outside world" and "at the same time . . . withdraws libidinal interests from his loved objects: so long as he suffers, he ceases to love."[11] In other words, where suffering, pain, and "increased tension" center the energy of the ego on itself, this very self-concern inhibits, diminishes, and ultimately negates concern for others. He further indicates "that the process which detaches the libido from its objects and blocks the way back to them again is closely allied to the process of repression."[12] The forcible process that provokes the withdrawal creates such anxiety that the process is repressed. He points to the formation of an "ego ideal" as the condition of repression. This ego ideal "deems itself the possessor of all perfections" and watches the ego and measures it according to its values and standards. On the one hand, the "self-regard is exalted"—as we have heard all religions, East and West, say of pride—while on the other hand, as Laing suggested, the self feels painfully *self-conscious*. In either case, self-preoccupation or self-absorption is apparent. But, more seriously, Freud finds that the superego becomes a "gathering-place for the death instincts."[13] A "displacement, a turning around upon his own ego," takes place as the narcissist, striving to control his aggressiveness toward the outer world, turns his aggressiveness toward his own ego. Freud explained this phenomenon, at least in part, in his paper on melancholia: "If the object love, which cannot be given up, takes refuge in narcissistic identification, while the object itself is abandoned, then hate is expended on this new substitute object . . . depreciating it, making it suffer and deriving sadistic gratification from its suffering."[14] Self-punishment is the devious way of taking revenge on the original object. Illness develops, "so as to avoid the necessity of openly expressing hostility against the loved ones."[15] This self-destructive aspect of narcissism brings us back to Narcissus as he "loved" himself to death. Now we begin to see the other half of the image of Narcissus. As Freud wrote: "It is this sadism . . . that solves the riddle of the tendency to suicide."[16]

As Freud's analysis of melancholia indicates, there is a *fate worse than death*, as we suggested originally, the fate of abandonment and lovelessness. In Freud's view, "to the ego, . . . living means the same as being loved."[17] To find itself unloved is not so much a fear of death as it is a fear *for* life. In such dread, the self falls and descends into nonbeing.

Freud considered fear of separation from the protecting mother and its consequent helplessness as the primordial danger situation. When such an experience actually takes place, it is "traumatic." Anxiety, the original response, is reproduced later in reaction to any dangerous situation that suggests that the trauma might be repeated. In a "traumatic situation in which the subject is helpless, external and internal dangers, real and instinctual, . . . converge."[18] According to Freud, then, anxiety is traceable to a "single situation, namely that of missing someone who is loved and longed for."[19] Longing turns into anxiety, lowers self-regard, and turns the self inward against itself. If the self "sees itself deserted by all protecting forces,"[20] abandoned and loveless, it lets itself die. Freud has thrown light on the narcissistic tendency in telling us that the self withdraws from and at the same time identifies with the loved and hated lost object and then hates itself. Yet the question remains as to how the self functions in this way and if a resolution to the problem exists. Freud himself said that all he had been able to do was to "peep over the wall of narcissism."[21] He concluded that this is the place where further advances in psychoanalysis will be made.

The Emerging Model of Man

The developing post-Freudian views are contributing to an emerging model of man.

There seems something strangely destructive . . . about us; something awry at the source. But perhaps it need not be so awry, perhaps if we better understood the making of love we might lessen our destructiveness. And it is here that psychoanalysis seems to offer us insights . . . relevant to our peace . . . psychoanalysis that takes us sufficiently deeply into the often hidden distortions, the retreats and regressions, the sicknesses, defenses and pretenses that attend upon the frustrations of the human heart.[22]

According to these views, something has gone wrong in man's original nexus that accounts for his tendency to pride, and its fatality. The infant has barely emerged from the womb when the state of dreaming innocence, as Kierkegaard called it, comes to an abrupt end, it is thought, by virtue of a frustrating, naysaying, word of prohibition. Freud traced the problem back to the trauma of separation. And, according to psychoanalytic theories that have developed more recently, the infant experiences limit situations, which differentiate self and not-self, in the deprivation and frustration of a need or needs.

This is inevitable and, in fact, essential. It defines self and world and makes possible the independent life of the individual. But if things go awry, this differentiation is aborted or distorted and relationships with others are affected accordingly. Although psychoanalytic theorists differ on the nature of the need and the dynamics of the distortion of the relationships,[23] they agree in recognizing the link between need and frustration in the child's first relationships to others. The physically and mentally impotent infant is needy and dependent— a potentially alarming situation that threatens annihilation even to an only awakening consciousness. The frustrating experience of unmet needs is met by the infant with helpless rage, heard in the baby's screaming and seen in its thrashing. In fact, it has been reported[24] that when infants are deserted by the loving and protecting forces—for, obviously, more is needed than food—they have let themselves die. "When disappointment and fury of revenge engenders such hatred . . . of life, . . . that life itself . . . is rejected."[25] This side of that extreme, there is surely a developing ambivalence—love/hatred of the other. This ambivalence—with its echo of Kierkegaard's "sympathetic antipathy" and Laing's view of the double bind—can be diminished by "proofs to [the infant] that the loved object . . . is not injured, is not turned into a vengeful person," whereas "lack of happy and close contact with loved people increases ambivalence, diminishes trust and hope and confirms anxieties about inner annihilation and external persecution."[26] In this dreadful state and in the helplessness of infancy the Fall occurs, as Kierkegaard put it. In this, man goes awry at the source, ontogenetically as well as phylogenetically. The self will not—cannot—become itself. It descends into nonbeing as a strategy for survival that fails. It becomes seemingly "independent" as a defense against dependence and unloving as a defense against rage. Without the mothering one's loving eyes, which lead to a "sense of self," the relationship between self and other goes awry.[27]

Psychological research in the last thirty years has moved back beyond the oedipal era, the era of father, and beyond

Oedipus as a model for self-understanding. It has moved into the preverbal, preoedipal period, the era of the mothering one and the infant—to get a glimpse over the "wall of narcissism." It looks into the important "field of work" that Freud said "still awaits exploration": the "disturbances to which the original narcissism of the child is exposed, the reactions with which he seeks to protect himself from them, the paths into which he is thereby forced."[28] It is not possible in this limited space to do justice to the development of psychoanalytic thought over the last thirty to fifty years.[29] It is useful, however, to indicate two significant developments of post-Freudian thought that have led to the research on narcissism and changes in psychoanalytic theory: the emphasis on the role of aggression (as distinct from Freud's emphasis on the sexual) in the personality as represented in the theories of Melanie Klein and her school of thought, and the development of an understanding of "object relations" (differing from Freud's concern with intrapsychic relations) as represented in the thought of Ronald Fairbairn and the "object relations" school.

Melanie Klein,[30] closely following Freud's libido theory, points to the period prior to three months of age as the time when what she calls the "depressive position" is established. Relics, at least, of this position remain always as an aberration in the individual's relation to himself and to others. She explains the disturbance at the source. The primal anxiety is the infant's fear of destroying the frustrating, "bad object" that he experiences the mother to be—yet, on whom he is dependent. Klein finds this to be the origin of the depressive position, for the self is then experienced as bad, guilty, and worthless. Feelings of unworthiness are rooted in this unconscious feeling of guilt. The need for praise and approval is grounded in the need to feel lovable in the face of aggressive impulses toward loved objects. The narcissistic preoccupation with the self in this view lies not in self-love but in underlying feelings of unworthiness and the need to feel worthy and lovable. Classical psychoanalysis does not in this sense go to the roots of man's tendency to go astray, for it does not deal with aggression in its archaic form in the infant's initial object relations. In her theoretical formulations, Klein opened up the importance of the preoedipal period—the period of narcissism.

Fairbairn, the Scottish psychiatrist, departed from Freud's libido theory. He wrote, in 1952, that "the point had now been reached at which, in the interest of progress, the classic libido theory would have to be transformed into a theory of development based essentially on object relationships."[31] He agreed with Klein on the importance of the primary infant/mother relationship. There is, however, a difference: Fairbairn's theory leaves behind Freud's primary emphasis on libido as seeking satisfaction and so being the driving force of the self, and stresses in its place the idea of the ego seeking object relations. There is a further difference in their understanding of the dynamics of deprivation and frustration. Freud and Melanie Klein following him have developed their views on the basis of a depressive position. By contrast, Fairbairn says "it is the schizoid position that constitutes the basis of the theory of mental structure" which he proposes. In the early oral phase the infant's *love* is felt as destructive and it is this that Fairbairn believes underlies the schizoid state. In a later oral phase of development it is the fear that one's *hate* is destructive that underlies and provides the basis for the depressive position.

In his view, the "great problem of the schizoid individual is how to love without destroying by love, whereas the great problem of the depressive individual is how to love without destroying by hate."[32] In his life relationships, the schizoid person will feel that his love is destructive and will avoid relationships of any depth that might elicit it. The depressive individual will become unable to direct love toward others without fear of directing also the hatred with which it is bound up. "The traumatic situation in either case is one in which the child feels that he is not really loved as a person and that his own love is not accepted."[33] In other words, either the individual feels his love is destructive or he feels rejected and unworthy because of the destructiveness of his hatred. Like Narcissus, he is in either case loveless and abandoned and in the absence of the assurance that he is loved his "relationship to objects is fraught with *too much anxiety over separation* to enable him to renounce the attitude of infantile dependence."

So, like Narcissus, the individual attempts to undo ego separation. Defensive techniques, Fairbairn writes, are meant to avoid the schizoid or depressive states that follow upon the traumatic loss of ego or the loss of object. Since everyone goes through the early and late oral phases of infancy, Fairbairn believes that there is a *universal tendency* to schizoid or depressive responses.[34] He expressed his belief that "everybody without exception must be regarded as schizoid." Since no one has a perfectly integrated ego, no one has emerged from the earliest periods of infancy unscathed.[35] It is then not a question of the existence of narcissism, but rather the degree.

In place of the Freudian ego/superego/id structure, Fairbairn postulates a multiplicity of egos: a central ego or "I"; a libidinal ego; and an aggressive persecutory ego, which he calls the "internal saboteur."[36] The internal saboteur is the agency within the self that reflects the infant's experience of rejection by the mothering one and reflects the self as an unloved, unworthy, bad self.[37] The experience of rejection by the mother of the self as bad, unloved, and worthless is repressed. The memory is lost. Patients often say, "I can't remember anything of my childhood experience." But the saboteur remains internalized and itself repressed as an aggressive persecutory ego to remind the self of its presumed unworthiness. The aggression is directed *primarily* against the object that is repressed and to which the ego is attached, and *secondarily* against the ego that incorporates it—within which it is contained. The result is self-destruction since the object is internalized within the self. He concludes that "the dynamic of repression is aggression"[38] and that the splitting of the ego—the schizoid self—is the result of this dynamic. "The splitting of the ego observed in the schizoid position is due to the operation of certain volume of aggression. . . . It is this aggression that provides the dynamic of the severance of the subsidiary egos from the central ego."[39] Both object and self are bad, since distinctions are obliterated in this negative narcissistic state. Again self is all—but a terrifying all, against which the self must defend itself and which must be protected against the self. As a consequence of this condition, seeing himself always through rejecting eyes and measuring himself always against impossible and unattainable ideals, "the unforgiven narcissist must sink to his death in his inability . . . to be the reconciled acceptable self."[40] Psychotherapy then must aim not simply at the resolution of conflict, but at a regrowth of the whole self.

In the light of Fairbairn's theory of multiple egos, it is possible, for instance, to speak of true and false selves, empirical and noumenal selves, without straying far from clinical reality. It is possible to speak of narcissism as a universal condition, since it is the level of the *universal schizoid position.* It is a metaphor for the rejection of love and for the dividedness in all of us. "[The schizoid personality] . . . keeps his love shut-in because he feels that it is too dangerous to release upon his objects."[41] His love is felt as destructive. On that same basis, he also protects himself against the love of others. Like Narcissus, who rejected all suitors, he renounces social contacts and withdraws into himself because he "must neither love nor be loved."

This self-enclosure is Kierkegaard's and Laing's demonic shut-upness. Man's tendency to pride, to narcissism, that seeming self-love, originates in the depth of anxiety, of dread, against which he devises a strategy for survival: he makes himself or attempts to make himself self-contained. But just as such love is false, so it is a false independence. Self is all—again— but in a twisted fashion. In place of true ego boundaries, the self lives in a defensive enclosure behind the "stone wall of narcissism" where it can still feel that all is self and objects are obliterated in a seeming "arrogant self-sufficiency." But it is an empty fortress from which there is no egress.

We see from what we have learned from Eastern sacred literature and from the Western Biblical tradition, as well as from psychoanalytic insights, that the diagnosis of our situation of East and West is similiar. Man's tendency to egoism—

egotheism—is self-destructive, it is *avidyā*, it is "original sin." Man's fall is a fall into inauthenticity, which means a fall into nonbeing. Psychoanalytic research has told us in a contemporary idiom what theological understanding has known over the centuries: that in response to the frustrating word and threat of punishment, in fear of rejection and abandonment, in impotence, the Fall occurs. Psychoanalysis has specified it further by tracing this to repressed aggression, which is directed against the self. But why is this so? What is the stone wall of narcissism? Can it be scaled?

Scaling the Stone Wall

The ingenious, often profound interpretations of the phenomenology of the condition [schizophrenia] would fill many volumes, but the forces that generated it are rarely discussed in these studies. This is not surprising. To reconstruct an ego by examining the products of its splitting or eventual disintegration is analogous to reassembling a plane from the debris scattered by its explosion. Granted that many people in psychotic states of schizophrenia seemed to be all wrapped up in themselves, why had they withdrawn their interest from the environment in the first place?[42]

Here we are speaking not only of schizophrenic hospitalized patients but of the schizoid condition in all of us. In the schizophrenia of the human spirit we all participate in differing degrees, just as theology tells us that every man is a "sinner." What path of liberation is there from narcissistic self-enclosure? How can one treat a condition that is preverbal, prelogical, prerational with the classical "talking cure" or with any kind of interpretation designed to give insight? Is man's narcissism accessible to treatment? Freud said no, since no transference can be effected because libido has been withdrawn from external objects and resistance is insuperable. This set limits to psychoanalysis. "Subsequent investigations have tended to confirm that . . . [the stone wall of narcissism] cannot be toppled by the customary analytic method without endangering the personality behind the wall."[43] But it is now considered to be a reversible process, by other methods. Donald Winnicott, the British psychiatrist, has pointed out that the patients who have been disturbed from the beginning call for "management"[44]—not classical analysis. For they lack a sense of self, a sense of their own being, the fundamental ontological need. Accordingly, Winnicott "distinguished between 'psychoanalysis' for 'oedipal cases' and 'management' for 'pre-oedipal cases.' "[45] Modern psychoanalytic theory, as developed by the American psychiatrist Hyman Spotnitz, is in accord with the view that classical analysis is not the appropriate method of treatment for preoedipal cases. "In essence," as Spotnitz observes, ". . . the approach which we delineate constitutes an outflanking of the wall, thus enabling it to stand and continue to fulfill its defensive function until the patient has outgrown the need for its protection."[46]

The outflanking maneuver recognizes the necessity of, indeed the value of, self-enclosure of the narcissistic individual and his inability to transfer feelings that he had for significant "objects" in his early life. Modern analysis depends on what is described as the narcissistic transference. (This is distinguished from object transference, for in the narcissistic transference the analyst functions as a narcissistic object or image to facilitate a duplication of the undifferentiated self/not-self environment.) In this environment, the patient's "wall" can be scaled or outflanked. The narcissistic patterns of resistance eventually can be resolved, by modes of communication other than object transference, which is not possible, and objective, rational interpretation to which resistance will not yield. Resistance to making conscious the unconscious is understood in the narcissistic disorders rather to be significant in terms of communication and to indicate the need for emotional reeducation. The goal of treatment is therefore "broadened to cover whatever obstacles to personality growth become manifest in the treatment relationship."[47] But Spotnitz has pointed out that "although the classical technique does not . . . resolve the basic problem in these cases . . ., a purely intuitive approach is undesirable. . . . Objective formulations . . . suggest effective treatment procedures.... Unless the practitioner has some way of taking readings of progress at each stage ... it is impossible to determine the degree of reversal of the schizophrenic reaction . . . and, later, whether the patient has been properly immunized against its return."[48]

The hypothesis on which modern analytic theory is based is that "the fundamental problem of the pathologically narcissistic patient is the destructive drive,"[49] and that the narcissistic defense inhibits aggressive behavior, although at the expense of the ego. The "polarity that figures significantly in the narcissistic defense is self-hatred and object love. The treatment is based on this working hypothesis."[50] Narcissistic disturbances are seen to be the response to the poisonous, destructive containment of negative feelings related to frustrating maturational factors, rather than repressed sexual feelings associated with the oedipal disorders. Thus a different but closely observed and evaluated approach is required. The traditional method of responding to the transference resistance of the neurotic, whose problems are understood to be rooted in a later verbal phase of development, is by verbal communication and interpretation which leads to *insight* in the patient and intellectual identification between analyst and patient.[51]

When these traditional methods were applied in cases of schizophrenia they were not effective. This was because a schizophrenic patient develops a hostile negative transference instead of a positive one. The schizoid person wants symbolically to destroy the analyst. Furthermore, it is not sexual repression that is central to the problem but rather the self-destructive repression of *aggressive* impulses that cause schizoid problems. Consequently, it is believed that contrary to Freud's understanding a state of negative transference can be therapeutically useful. "It is now recognized that hatred can be a therapeutic force. Many analysts have reported this discovery. Hatred binds the schizoid patient to his transference object even more firmly than love. *He is willing to work as long as necessary to master his aggressive impulses provided that the danger that he will act on them destructively is kept to a mini-*

mum."[52] Thus the focus of therapy is to remove obstacles to the expression of hostility, but barriers are put up against acting on destructive urges. This is accomplished by regulating the degree of tension to which the patient is exposed while establishing a treatment atmosphere that makes it possible for him to verbalize rather than to act on aggressive impulses. Although the therapist's inclination is to respond to the suffering of the individual with warmth and kindness, *this would not* be beneficial to the patient who feels so threatened by closeness to the other person that he has enclosed himself behind an almost impregnable defense.[53] The core problem is that rage, felt by the infant in response to an environment that failed to meet his maturational needs and in which the ecology of the self was disturbed, was turned back on the self. It is here at the source that we go astray, as Kierkegaard and Laing have told us. The "object field of the mind was obliterated to protect the external object against the discharge of destructive impulsivity. . . . Running away psychologically from hostile impulses into non-feeling stares and self preoccupations eventually becomes a compulsive operation."[54] The "self-hatred . . . has to be unmasked, transformed into object-hatred, and steadily tapped off"[55] and released toward the analyst until transformed.

Responding to the narcissistic patient with the usual warmth and kindness would, as Spotnitz observes, "block the release of the poison that sickened him and drive him toward permanent deteriorated schizophrenia."[56] Since schizoid characteristics are universal in this era,[57] a premature closeness with any patient would be detrimental to his treatment. Narcissistic disorders require this form of initial treatment in all cases. The hostility that has been directed against himself in the protection of the loved/hated object must gradually be released and deflected onto the therapeutic partner in the analytic relationship. This is based on a slow process of *verbal communication* in order to deter any aggressive behavior, as well as to protect the patient from further self-attack, which would lead to further fragmentation of the ego and psychosis. To promote this kind of treatment, the narcissistic defense is supported and encouraged until it can be safely lowered. "Resistances are handled in an entirely different way than that dictated by standard procedure. The patient is not put under any pressure to overcome them; as a matter of fact, he is helped to preserve his resistances . . . because of their insulative value."[58] His resistance to communication is "joined" on the theory that if you cannot beat them, join them.[59]

The patient is encouraged to talk—to "tell the story of his life"—and his resistances to doing so are studied rather than interpreted, which the narcissistic person would construe as an attack. Eventually the patient will "contact" the therapist, perhaps by asking a question, and this is responded to in a manner that will foster a "narcissistic transference"; that is, one in which the person feels the analyst is like him. He "is permitted to mold the transference object in his own image"[60] so that he will be free to feel both love and hate—love for the likeness reflected, the rapport established, and the empathy and understanding he receives. The patient will also be free to feel hate for his therapist just as he hates himself. (His egocentricity is encouraged!) The treatment allows the patient, like Narcissus, to bask in the reflection of his own image. The focus remains on the negative aspects of the transference in order to prevent action based on impulses and to drain off the hateful "toxins" that have poisoned the individual.[61] Verbal expression of negative feelings relieves the need to act on them. Various responses are used to treat narcissistic patterns.[62] Psychological reflection is used to resolve the defense pattern of attack by the "worthless" self on itself, that is, devaluation of the self and overvaluation of the object. This echoing of the ego is a therapeutic strategy used to reflect back to the individual his pattern of self-attack and yet the analyst never abandons this "worthless" self. This is intended to repeat the disturbing pattern of the individual's relationships but in the therapeutic context in which the therapist serves as the object, a target for the ego's aggressive impulses. Sooner or later the psychological twin image, which faithfully stands by and joins in the ego's attack upon itself, arouses sufficient resentment to reverse the flow of mobilized aggression from the ego to the object. The therapist's attitude is one of acceptance of the verbal aggression.

⌈Another mode of reflecting the ego's pattern of self-attack and feelings of worthlessness involves "devaluating the object." Instead of echoing the ego's low regard of the self, the therapist lets the patient know that he, too, is worthless in order to resolve the defense of object worship that makes it impossible for him to ventilate his hostility at the risk of losing the valuable object (the original reason for the containment of anger). Instead of presenting himself as an object of worship that one cannot afford to offend, or as one with superior knowledge that the patient comes to tap, the therapist presents himself as *like* the patient and therefore worthy of attack. Again, this makes possible the deflection of hostility from the self to the object.

In this manner the therapist eventually helps the person to deal with his early, disturbed interpersonal relationships. It is postulated that in those beginnings when self and not-self were relatively undifferentiated, hostile impulses were activated in response to inevitable frustration. The self went astray. It established defenses that now operate in the treatment relationship. The analyst duplicates that situation, and in so doing, self and other become confused, and ultimately merge. In the presence of that undisturbing sameness, understanding, and rapport, the patient feels free to come out from behind the "stone wall" and speak his feelings. Psychological reflection thus facilitates the resolution and transformation of those defensive patterns. They are joined, supported, and encouraged until the patient no longer needs them. In this fashion, the wall is outflanked. The negative narcissistic transference made possible by the methods that have been briefly sketched becomes the way out of the fortress for the encapsulated self. The goal of modern psychoanalysis is, by thus lifting the stone of self-hatred, to restore the ability to love and be loved, to encourage mutual love. It is this capacity that Narcissus, reflecting our own condition, so tragically lacked. The implication for human relationships in general is certainly not to encourage reciprocal anger or hatred as a first step toward reciprocal loving. It is rather to encourage a transformation that would make it possible to recognize the existence of those negative feelings. It is *repressed* anger and hatred turned back on the self that functions as an obstacle to proper self-love as well as love of an other. In this lies our tendency to "pride" and its destructiveness. It is with these unacknowledged feelings that we make war while we speak peace, and do violence with our apparent love. In fact, we may be unwittingly arranging our "fearful end," as did Narcissus.

Schizophrenia, the narcissistic disorder par excellence, informs us about ourselves. For as Fairbairn had in fact said, we are all schizoid.[63] Fromm says we suffer from a "pathology of normalcy," a "chronic low-grade schizophrenia."[64] Ernest Becker goes farther and suggests that this is an exaggerated form of the human condition: "Schizophrenia takes the risk of evolution to its furthest point in man. . . . This is really a cursed animal in evolution, an animal gone astray beyond natural limits. . . . Man alone achieves this terrifying condition which we see in all its purity at the extremes of schizophrenic psychosis."[65] Although he is emphasizing the mind/body aspects of the problem, the generalization nevertheless holds: "The psychoses are a caricature of the life-styles of all of us—which is probably part of the reason that they make us so uncomfortable."

Beyond the Wall

Many have now said that "neurosis is another word for the total problem of the human condition. . . . Men are naturally neurotic and always have been. . . . Modern man lives his contradictions for the worse. . . . There is no embracing world view for the neurotic to depend on or merge with to mask his problems and so the 'cure' for neurosis is difficult in our time."[66] Not only is the cure difficult in our time, or in any, but what is significant is that we now know the condition for what it is. Today we recognize that we have not merely to deal with neurosis and hysteria, the conditions that were identified in Freud's time, but we are aware that we have to deal with narcissism in its extreme form—the exaggerated condition of schizophrenia. It is this condition, the stone wall of the encapsulated self, that has until recently been considered *not* amenable to treatment. We have cultural schizophrenia to confront, a situation that is compounded by our contemporary cultural bankruptcy to be sure, by "feeling as sinners without the religious belief in sin," which "aggravates the problem of [man's] separateness and hyperconsciousness."[67] That has been precisely our point. While we have lost our belief in sin and traditional modes of self-understanding the message of modern psychoanalytic thought resonates with that of our traditions. It points to Narcissus—reconsidered—as a post-Freudian model for our self-understanding. It teaches ancient wisdom in a contemporary idiom and therefore may speak to us as our traditional mythos no longer seems to do. Modern psychoanalytic thought indicates that what has been viewed as sin has been a defensive mode of being devised to survive our separateness. What we know now suggests that, "feeling as sinners," unworthy and loveless, we wrap ourselves in self "love." Now we know that the disturbance at the source, as expressed in the story of the fall of man and in descriptions of the original motive of the infant, leaves us abandoned and "in exile." It is the ground of our narcissism.

Surely then there is good reason why we should look again into the roots of this "consciousness of sin," as Kierkegaard called it, to see where we have gone astray and how we have been self-destructive. There is even more reason why we should attempt to regain the path, to reverse our direction, to alleviate our existential predicament, no matter how "impossible" that may appear. We know why we have not been doing so. Theologians have told us that we move in a negative direction to grace. Sin is a rejection of grace. We move opposite to the Tao and defy our own natures. We have a mysterious tendency to falsify our relation to reality—Avidya. What we now learn from modern psychoanalytic research is a similar message: Narcissism is a mask to disguise our predicament and a resistance to self-transcendence—a resistance whose resolution is not an easy matter. As Freud told us, psychoanalysis is not a cure-all. Certainly psychology does not offer salvation and we have learned from a long religious tradition that there is no salvation within history. We are in accord with Philip Rieff:[68] this has been an era in which "psychological man"—that is, man as narcissist, self-preoccupied and concerned with his individual intrapsychic drama between ego, id, and superego—has finally and clearly emerged. However, as Laing says, man has to be understood within relevant contextual systems. Bateson says that man must be understood in his social matrix.[69]

We do not agree that the interests of psychoanalysis are not consonant with those of religion. On the contrary, it seems clear that the modern psychoanalytic model not only informs the Eastern and Western religious models of man but indicates their common denominator in the image of Narcissus, as a paradigm for man's isolation and self-destructiveness. It also suggests a mode of egress from our narcissistic self-enclosure, from the hell of the isolated individual consciousness. In so doing, it confirms the goals of our ancient religious traditions. It suggests the possibility of the resolution of the resistance to relatedness to others—to self-transcendence. Ernest Becker, Philip Rieff, and Norman O. Brown are among those who say that psychology has to give way to theology. Perhaps psychology has to *lead* the way *back* to theology, as Tillich thought. Modern psychoanalytic thought may be a step in that direction. It points the way to resolving our resistance to transcendence, to overcoming the "complete isolation of the individual," helping us to be open to "hearing the words" of our traditions. It may at the very least give us some understanding of the sense of unworthiness that is at the heart of our condition. Our dread of a fate worse than death, which forces our self-enclosure, is the dread of being abandoned and loveless in these "infinite spaces" and the fear that our rage might out. There is a profound truth in what we have long been told by the major religious traditions—that we have strayed from the path and become separated from our Source. At best we might learn individually and collectively to be "educated by dread" to eradicate it and so avoid perpetuating the terror of "love's defeat" that drives us all to isolate ourselves, partially or totally, even as Narcissus did. We might even learn mutual love.

Modern psychoanalysis is concerned with the individual's relatedness to others. When freed for that relatedness, the individual is freed for the traditional ideals of love, faith, and compassion. This is obviously not possible if one feels worthless, and worse than that, if one is destructive of oneself and others. Psychoanalysis works in the service of freedom to respond to and relate to others, to love, to choose values. It aims to unbind the will and to make possible the coincidence of our conscious and unconscious intentions. It intends to help us to have the "courage to be" in the face of the terror of meaninglessness, and perhaps even to restore meaning by making egress into the meaningful possible. This is no small task today, nor has it ever been.

7

Resolution

> If Master K'ung was right, we must indeed all be teachers, we
> must practise and cherish the old in order to discover the new;
> and in attaining the new, we indeed reanimate the old.
>
> *Herbert Fingarette*[1]

THE IMAGE of Narcissus links sin and madness, the old and
the new, across the centuries, reflecting the traditional wisdom
of the East and the West, and leading to a post-Freudian
model of man on which we may build with a new understanding of where we have gone astray. For Narcissus mirrors back
to us our strange condition. In the East, despite our cultural
differences, we found in the sacred literature of India, China,
and Japan that the structure of the human condition, the
nature of the fundamental human reality, and man's relationship to existence are seen in a similar way. Only the images
differ, since they are culturally determined. However, the struc-
tural relationship of the symbols permits exchanges between
them. The diagnosis of the core problem of human existence
in the religions of the East is understood to be a pathology of
self-centeredness—isolation in ignorance from true reality. In
the West that pathology of self-centeredness is known as pride.
All religions address themselves to man's human response to
his human predicament, to man's narcissism and attempt to
overcome it. One can even speculate that they may originally
have arisen in response to his dread of separation and abandon-

ment, to his need to heal the breach between himself and his source—to regain attachment.

Now that we have explored our tendency to narcissism and its self-destructiveness, let us look again at the paths of transformation, old and new. We have considered (in Chapter 3) the similarity between the views of Kierkegaard and Laing, and the connections between sin and madness. We find not only similar diagnoses but remarkable resemblances as well between Kierkegaard's Christian therapeutic and the modern psychoanalytic therapy outlined by Spotnitz. For both Kierkegaard and the modern analysts, communication plays a central role in the therapy. Kierkegaard distinguished between direct and indirect communication for therapeutic purposes. He used indirect communication as a "calculated trap" to lure the reader into self-recognition and to dispel illusions. Kierkegaard advocated going along with the self, saying, "One begins by accepting the other man's illusion as good money,"[2] just as modern analysts do. In its version of Freud's "talking cure," modern analysis joins and mirrors the ego in the narcissistic transference. It uses psychological reflection to lure the person into eventual self-recognition, thus encouraging and making possible the emergence from behind the wall of narcissism and reversing the direction of the self-aggression. Ultimately, as with Kierkegaard, direct communication is possible. In the therapeutic mode of indirect communication, the therapist, the communicator, is reduced to being "nobody," as Kierkegaard said.[3] When the illusions have been dispelled, then the relationship between communicator and listener is what matters. This is true also in the therapeutic model of modern analysis (as distinct from classical analysis) in which the realistically induced feelings, the countertransference, of the analyst are used therapeutically in the relationship with the individual and, additionally, in modeling behavior for the patient.[4] In both instances progress is measured by the flow of communication. Kierkegaard describes the "demonic" as the silent, while the self that is able to be in relation to an other he describes as transparent. Modern analysis measures therapeutic movement by means of progressive communication. Resistance is indicated by interruption of the flow of communication.

For Kierkegaard, the first movement of the spirit, resignation of the old self, is a painful process, the essential expression of which is "suffering." For modern analysis, the giving way of defenses—resistance—is equally painful, but for both it is a necessary step. The acceptance of forgiveness, the acceptance of oneself as cared for, is a final step. Recollection backward, Kierkegaard said, is insufficient for authentic existence; the "repetition" of one's lost existential possibility is required for cure. Modern analysis also seeks to evoke the past but to remember it in the present in order to repeat, in the therapeutic situation, the patterns in the relationship between self and others that have been distorted. As Kierkegaard wrote, *"existential appropriation"* of knowledge is necessary because faith is a medium of "passion." As modern analysis says, resolution of resistance is what is sought—an existential resolution via maturational interpretation—not insight via rational interpretation. The goal is not merely intellectual understanding but personal transformation. It is recognized that knowing the "good" is not sufficient for doing it. For Kierkegaard what intervenes is will; for modern and classical analysis the intervening factor is resistance. Both, however, recognize the need to go along initially with the negative willing—the resistance —to bring it to complete despair before it will be relinquished, freeing the individual from the prison of egocentricity into relationship with an other.

Kierkegaard said that his intent was to "nudge" his readers into becoming themselves, specifically into becoming themselves as Christians. Modern analytic therapy aims to "nudge" those who indicate a desire for change into becoming themselves—"a journey of self-discovery"[5] into maturity as human beings so that they can choose what they want to be on their own path.

There are no specifically religious value judgments in modern analytic therapy as, for instance, in Kierkegaard's Christian therapeutic. Modern psychoanalysis is, as we have said, chiefly a mode of freeing one to be able to *choose* values rather than to remain compulsively bound in defensive patterns. Within this concept of maturity, "becoming who you are," in Nietzsche's paradoxical phrase, or Socrates' "Know thyself," or the Zen master's request to show the face you had before you were born, lies the traditional wisdom of the human heritage. The goal is a *restitutio ad integram.*

As we have tried to indicate, religious wisdom has suggested that what is "wrong" with man is his egocentricity and that his salvation lies in self-transcendence. All the religions with a natural cosmic orientation seek a form of "return" to an original unity (not regressive, but self-transcending). The historically oriented religions recognize the polarity of distance and relation and urge a restoration of relationship, as distinct from unity. This understanding is universal, whether "other" is understood as Other, as in the God of the historical personal religions where harmony with the will of God is sought, or whether "alteration" (othering, to use Laing's term), or transformation of the individual is sought, as in the Eastern tradition.

One might argue that it matters to which "other" one is related—the God of the Judeo-Christian tradition or the Taoist natural order, the Confucian moral order, or the Hindu Brahman. The point of the path of liberation in each, however, is to free one for relatedness of self to other—to free one for self-transcendence in a particular cultural context. Whether the sage is called Sunnyasin, Arahat, Bodhisattva, or saint, he represents or symbolizes a similar core of fundamental human values. The sages may be clothed in significant cultural differences and emphasize different aspects of our humanity, but what is common to all is the emphasis on egress from ego and the need for self-transcendence.

Awakening to this new recognition of connectedness or relatedness is the goal of modern analytic therapy just as this awakening is the goal of Eastern religious disciplines. Freud himself, in the *Introductory Lectures,* relates the goal of mystical practices to bring about the transformation of personality to that of psychoanalysis in which knowledge leads also to transformation. The mode of arriving at this knowledge was for Freud a way of free association, or making the unconscious conscious, to release man from the "ignorance" *(avidyā)* of his relation to his environment, to reality, the world. Man suffers from encapsulation in an egoic mode of experience that is maya, a veil of illusion, as Laing said, and it is this "nonproblem" from which he must be released and about which he needs enlightenment. He is trapped in samsara—the "vicious circle of self-frustrating activity"[6]—from which the various ways of liberation propose release. When enlightened as to his true condition, man will know this (existentially, not theoretically) by being a transformed being whose existence is in harmony with the cosmos.

What is sought is not the "regressive" unity of a return to a lost Eden but the consciousness of participation in reality that lies beyond an awareness of separation—what Owen Barfield has called final participation.[7] The names of the goal are many: recognition of the essential relatedness of Atman/Brahman (self/Self) in Hindu thought, enlightenment in Buddhist thought, the Jen man in Confucian thought, harmony with the Tao in Taoism, relationship to God in the Biblical tradition, and for Plato, simply, to know the Good. As Fromm has pointed out, "The differences between the symbols are caused by the social and cultural differences existing in the various countries in which they arose,"[8] but the question regarding man's existence and the goal of the path, the regaining of attachment, (see Chapter 5, note 5), the overcoming of egocentricity, is the same. Not only do they speak for a transformed consciousness that would recognize relatedness but they agree that that cannot be willed and that coercion of reality by the self must cease. Storming the castle, attacking the narcissistic wall, either by the therapist or by conscious effort on the part of the patient, will be of no avail because defensive needs and unconscious intentions are moving in another direction. The concept of resistance is consonant with the idea of willfulness in the Biblical tradition and of disharmony of self and Self in the East. Hence the understanding of going along with the will of God in the Biblical tradition; of emptying the self—the Void—in Zen, and the resolution of the resistance in modern analysis.

The emerging of the self into reality takes place in the relationship of teacher/guru to disciple in all the cultures we have considered. *Upanishad* means sitting near a teacher. Bodhisattva is an enlightened one who leads others. Although in Freudian psychoanalysis the analyst is a detached objective observer, the modern analyst is a participant by way of his objective countertransference. The analyst lets the patient be and supports and respects his defenses. He helps the patient to resolve the resistances that block his growth. Just as the modern analyst acts indirectly as a maturational agent, so the Zen master acts according to a similar maturational method. Satori is an awakening to reality, a nonconceptual reception of reality, an insight into one's own nature—an experiential insight that is neither intellectual nor logical. Its "method consists in putting one in a dilemma out of which one must contrive to escape not through logic indeed but through a mind of higher order."[9] The method is a "calculated trap," as with Kierkegaard. The Zen master uses koans to puzzle his student, to drive him into a corner where no more questions can be asked but only an emotion experienced that may bring enlightenment—a lifting of an emotional block to "seeing." As a result, the problem with which one has been wrestling is suddenly "seen" as a false problem. The only way to extricate oneself from the double-bind situation, as Bateson conceptualized it and Laing described it, is to get out of that context, or out of that game into another in which the double bind no longer functions. But the third injunction of the double-bind situation is not to be aware that you are bound. We seem not to want "right sight" as Augustine put it. It is this resistance to a transformation of consciousness which the teachers of our traditions have tried by every means to resolve.

The sages—Eastern and Western—attempt to overcome our self-encapsulation through their paths of liberation by driving the individual out of his ordinary logical conceptual patterns into an experience that will transform his awareness. The screens through which we perceive the world with impaired vision must be lifted—the "mirror" polished. This is the timeless message of all the great religions and all the greatest thinkers. This is what history, understood as a means of restoring our consciousness, may help us to re-member. It may enable us to discover the wisdom of the new, while the new, modern analytic understanding of man may reanimate the old by specifying the root of our tendency to pride and its self-destructiveness, about which we have wondered for so long.[10] Eastern philosophers have inquired into the sources of our self-isolation as have those of the West; and there is, as this book has attempted to show, a remarkable congruence in their understanding of human reality, symbolized by the Greeks in the myth of Narcissus, in the Indian tradition by *avidyā*, the Chinese by *yu* (anxiety), portrayed by Kierkegaard as the "shut-up" self, by Laing as the divided self, and in modern psychoanalytic terminology as schizophrenia. The aim of the sages has been a transformation of consciousness that would reverse our self-destructiveness, make the self whole, and heal the split between self and other. As long as we do violence with our "love," to ourselves and others, the supreme injunction, Love thy neighbor as thyself, will be nothing but an ironic comment on our predicament. Like Narcissus, many of us have heard Echo. What we need to be able to do is to listen for something other than an Echo of the self—to hear a resonance between the self and others—and to respond.

Notes

PREFACE

1. Blaise Pascal, *Pensées*, tr. by W. F. Trotter, intro. by T. S. Eliot (E. P. Dutton & Co., Inc., 1958), #427.

2. Ronald D. Laing, *The Politics of Experience* (Pantheon Books, 1967), p. xv.

3. Robert L. Heilbroner, "The Human Prospect," *New York Review of Books*, Jan. 24, 1974, p. 34.

Chapter 1. NARCISSUS RECONSIDERED: THE MYTH

1. Ovid, *Metamorphosis*, Book III: *"Iste ego sum: sensi, nec me mea fallit imago; uror amore mei: flammas moveoque, feroque."*

2. Pascal, *Pensées*, #425.

3. Paul Ricoeur, *Symbolism of Evil*, tr. by Emerson Buchanan (Harper & Row, Publishers, Inc., 1967), p. 356.

4. *Ibid.*

5. Walter Kaufman, *Nietzsche* (Meridian Books, Inc., 1960), p. 81.

6. Ronald D. Laing, *Politics of Experience*, p. 99.

7. Wilhelm Pauck (tr. and ed.), *Luther: Lectures on Romans*, The Library of Christian Classics, Vol. XV (The Westminster Press, 1961).

8. Pascal, *Pensées*, #455.

9. *Ibid.*, #414.

10. *Ibid.*, #427.

11. Jacques Monod, *Chance and Necessity* (Alfred A. Knopf, Inc., 1971).

12. Ernest Becker, *The Denial of Death* (The Free Press, 1973), p. 2.

13. Sigmund Freud, *A General Introduction to Psychoanalysis*, tr. by Joan Riviere (Pocket Books, 1973), pp. 430–431. There are still resistances to dealing with studies of narcissism. See Lester Schwartz, "Techniques and Prognosis in the Treatment of Narcissistic Personality Disorders," *Journal of the American Psychoanalytic Association*, 1973, Vol. 21 (3), pp. 617–632. It is interesting to note that until 1973 there was no category listing for "narcissism" in *Psychology Abstracts*, for instance, and prior to that it was indexed as "self-love."

14. For this perspective, see Hyman Spotnitz and Phillip Resnikoff, "The

Myths of Narcissus," *The Psychoanalytic Review*, Vol. 41, No. 2 (April 1954).

15. The account that follows is taken mainly from Grace Stuart, *Narcissus* (London: George Allen & Unwin, Ltd., 1956).

16. Ovid, *Metamorphosis*, Book III.

17. Robert Graves, *The Greek Myths* (Penguin Books, Inc., 1961), pp. 286–288.

18. William Wordsworth, *Prélude* I, 55–56.

19. I am indebted to Owen Barfield for the clarification of these lines of the myth.

20. Ovid, *Metamorphosis*, Book III.

21. *Ibid.*

22. Spotnitz and Resnikoff, "The Myths of Narcissus," p. 177.

23. Sir James George Frazer, *The Golden Bough* (The Macmillan Company, 1894), Vol. 3, p. 94.

24. Photius, Byzantine scholar and Patriarch of Constantinople in A.D. 858–867 and 878–886.

25. Pausanius, *The Description of Greece*, tr. from the Greek by J. G. Frazer (Biblo & Tannen, 1965), Vol. V, Book IX–31.7.

26. Stuart, *Narcissus*, p. 21.

27. Robert Payne, *Hubris, A Study of Pride* (Harper & Brothers, Harper Torchbooks, 1960), p. 176.

28. Stuart, *Narcissus*, p. 24.

29. *Ibid.*, pp. 23–24.

30. *Ibid.*

31. Ovid, *Metamorphosis*, Book III.

32. John Hawkes, *The Lime Twig*, intro. by Leslie Fiedler (New Directions, 1961), p. ix.

33. Stuart, *Narcissus*, p. 41.

34. Payne, *Hubris, A Study of Pride*, p. 312.

35. Owen Barfield, *Poetic Diction*, 3d ed. with Afterword by the author (Wesleyan University Press, 1973), p. 223.

Chapter 2. SIN: THE FLIGHT FROM THE SELF

1. William Barrett, *Irrational Man* (Doubleday & Company, Inc., Anchor Books, 1958), p. 151.

2. Pauck (ed.), *Luther: Lectures on Romans*, p. 159.

3. Shirley Sugerman, "Sin and Madness: Flight from the Self," doctoral dissertation, Drew University, 1970. This book constitutes a further development of the concept of narcissism as originally articulated in the dissertation. See especially the conclusion, pp. 294–295; also, "Sin and Madness: Flight from the Self," *Cross Currents*, Vol. XXI, No. 2 (Spring 1971), pp. 129–153.

4. Søren Kierkegaard, *The Concept of Dread* (1844), tr. by Walter Lowrie

(Princeton University Press, 1944). Kierkegaard calls this book a "psychological deliberation oriented in the direction of . . . original sin." Self throughout is understood as subject, as the whole person, and is used, as is ego, to refer to the individual *(das Ich)*. When this is not so, because distinctions are necessary, qualifying terms such as true and false, noumenal and empirical, are employed. Ego is used in a technical sense only in the section of Chapter 6 on W. Ronald D. Fairbairn's thought, where it refers, as he does, to aspects of the psyche.

5. Søren Kierkegaard, *Fear and Trembling and The Sickness Unto Death* (1843 and 1849 respectively), tr. by Walter Lowrie; tr. revised by Howard A. Johnson (Doubleday & Company, Inc., Anchor Books, 1954).

6. Pauck (ed.), *Luther: Lectures on Romans,* p. 159.

7. Bruno Bettleheim, *The Empty Fortress* (The Free Press, 1967).

8. Pascal, *Pensées,* #434.

9. Martin Buber, *Between Man and Man,* tr. by R. G. Smith (London: Routledge & Kegan Paul, Ltd., 1947), p. 42.

10. That we seek death and destruction as much as life is a problem that presents itself variously in contemporary literature as loss of the self, the absurd self of Eugene Ionesco's plays, the amorphous beings in Samuel Beckett's plays, the tropisms in Nathalie Sarraute's novels, the sense of meaninglessness in Paul Tillich's writings, the isolated self of Sylvia Plath's *The Bell Jar,* the proliferating literature on violence, depression, suicide, all of which "reads like a fever chart for a bad case of melancholy" as Anne Sexton said of her poems in *Live or Die.* Our self-destructiveness manifests itself in contemporary society as an epidemic problem of depression, estimated to affect about eight million people.

11. Kierkegaard, *Concept of Dread,* p. 18. The quotations following are from pp. 37–55.

12. Kierkegaard, *Sickness Unto Death,* p. 167.

13. Kierkegaard, *Concept of Dread,* p. 55.

14. Kierkegaard, *Either/Or: A Fragment of Life* (1843), tr. by David F. and Lillian M. Swenson and Walter Lowrie, with a foreword by Howard A. Johnson (Doubleday & Company, Inc., Anchor Books, 1959), Vol. II, p. 173.

15. L. L. Whyte, in *The Unconscious Before Freud* (Basic Books, Inc., 1960), suggests that it is likely that the split between man and environment into subject and object occurred originally as a way of dealing with situations in which man felt endangered.

16. Kierkegaard, *Concept of Dread.* See pp. 105–121 for his analysis of the demoniacal personality.

17. Kierkegaard, *Sickness Unto Death,* pp. 239–240.

18. Kierkegaard, *Concept of Dread,* p. 110. His description of "shut-upness" can be found on pp. 110–118.

19. Kierkegaard, *Either/Or,* Vol. II, p. 193; see Emil Durkheim, *Suicide,* tr. by John A. Spaulding and George Simpson (Free Press, 1951), for his view

that suicide results from such introversion, from a lack of social cohesion and of community.

20. Stuart, *Narcissus,* p. 21.

21. Kierkegaard, *Sickness Unto Death,* p. 214.

22. Kierkegaard, *Concept of Dread,* p. 113, and for the following discussion, see pp. 111–115.

23. Kierkegaard, *Sickness Unto Death,* p. 207.

24. Kierkegaard, *Concept of Dread,* p. 111.

25. *Ibid.,* p. 111; and for a modern analytic view of this, see Evelyn Liegner, "The Silent Patient," *The Psychoanalytic Review,* Vol. 61, No. 2 (1974).

26. *Ibid.,* pp. 139–141 for discussion of healing via dread.

27. Søren Kierkegaard, *Philosophical Fragments, or a Fragment of Philosophy* (1844), tr. and intro. by David F. Swenson (Princeton University Press, 1944), p. 11. Note in Chapters 5 and 6 the striking similarity of views of Zen and modern analysis on communication.

28. Søren Kierkegaard, *Point of View for My Work as an Author* (1848), tr. by Walter Lowrie and ed. with preface by Benjamin Nelson (Harper & Row, Publishers, Inc., Harper Torchbooks, 1962), p. 40.

29. Søren Kierkegaard, *Concluding Unscientific Postscript to the Philosophical Fragments* (1846), tr. by David F. Swenson and completed and ed. by Walter Lowrie (Princeton University Press, 1941), pp. 74–79.

30. *Ibid.,* p. 78.

31. Søren Kierkegaard, *Training in Christianity* (1850), tr. by Walter Lowrie (Princeton University Press, 1944), p. 133. It is interesting to note that Pascal, Kierkegaard, and Laing all used the image of a "knot" to describe the human predicament.

32. Kierkegaard, *Concluding Unscientific Postscript,* p. 412.

33. Søren Kierkegaard, *Edifying Discourses,* tr. by David F. and Lillian M. Swenson and intro. by Paul L. Holmer (Harper & Brothers, Harper Torchbooks, 1958), p. 160; the ensuing quotations are from pp. 161–165.

Chapter 3. MADNESS: THE DIVIDED SELF

1. Hawkes, *The Lime Twig,* p. ix.

2. Ronald D. Laing, *The Divided Self: An Existential Study in Sanity and Madness,* 2d ed. (Penguin Books, Inc., 1966), p. 82.

3. *Ibid.,* pp. 73–74.

4. Laing, *Politics of Experience,* p. 3.

5. *Ibid.,* pp. 98–99.

6. Kierkegaard, *Concluding Unscientific Postscript,* p. 175.

7. Laing, *Divided Self,* p. 46.

8. *Ibid.,* pp. 39–41.

9. Ronald D. Laing, "Minkowski and Schizophrenia," *Review of Existen-*

tial Psychology and Psychiatry, Vol. II, No. 3 (1963), pp. 198–201; *Divided Self,* pp. 41–43.

10. Laing, *Politics of Experience,* p. xiv.

11. Ronald D. Laing, "An Examination of Tillich's Theory of Anxiety and Neurosis," *British Journal of Medical Psychology,* Vol. 31 (1958), pp. 88–89.

12. Laing, *Divided Self,* p. 93.

13. *Ibid.,* p. 92.

14. *Ibid.,* p. 57.

15. *Ibid.,* p. 51.

16. *Ibid.,* p. 38.

17. *Ibid.,* pp. 73–75.

18. *Ibid.,* p. 130.

19. *Ibid.,* p. 157.

20. Ronald D. Laing, *The Self and Others, Further Studies in Sanity and Madness* (London: Tavistock Publications, Ltd., 1961), p. 75.

21. *Ibid.,* p. ix.

22. Laing, *Divided Self,* p. 82.

23. Laing, *Self and Others,* p. 127.

24. Laing, *Divided Self,* p. 106.

25. *Ibid.,* p. 112.

26. Stuart, *Narcissus,* p. 46.

27. Laing, *Divided Self,* p. 116.

28. *Ibid.,* p. 117.

29. Stuart, *Narcissus,* p. 45.

30. Laing, *Self and Others,* pp. 131 ff.

31. Gregory Bateson; D. D. Jackson; J. Haley; and J. J. Weakland, "Towards a Theory of Schizophrenia," *Behavioral Science,* Vol. I, No. 4 (Oct., 1956).

32. Laing, *Politics of Experience,* p. 77.

33. Bateson; Jackson; Haley; and Weakland, "Towards a Theory of Schizophrenia," and see Gregory Bateson's *Steps to an Ecology of Mind* (Ballantine Books, 1972), p. 202, where he explains that different logical types are different levels of abstraction. He points out—as the basis of his theory of the double bind—that although in formal logic a discontinuity is maintained between the different levels, "in the psychology of real communication this discontinuity is. . . . breached," and that pathology occurs in the human organism when it occurs in certain patterns between mother and child.

34. Laing, *Politics of Experience,* pp. 78–79.

35. Kierkegaard, *Concept of Dread,* p. 41.

36. Laing, *Politics of Experience,* p. 32.

37. Laing, *Divided Self,* p. 104.

38. *Ibid.,* pp. 158–159.

39. Laing, *Self and Others,* p. 120.

40. Laing, *Divided Self,* p. 165.

41. *Ibid.,* p. 164.

42. Laing, *Politics of Experience,* p. 89.

43. *Ibid.,* p. 138.

44. *Ibid.,* p. 12.

45. *Ibid.,* p. 114.

46. *Ibid.,* p. 116.

47. *Ibid.,* p. 95.

48. *Ibid.,* p. 96.

49. *Ibid.,* pp. 98–99.

50. *Ibid.,* p. 49.

51. *Ibid.,* p. 101.

52. Barrett, *Irrational Man,* p. 248.

53. Laing, *Politics of Experience,* p. 70.

54. *Ibid.,* p. 82.

55. *Ibid.,* p. 83.

56. Laing, *Divided Self,* p. 77.

57. *Ibid.,* p. 74.

58. *Ibid.,* p. 93.

Chapter 4. Sin and Madness: A Transformation of Consciousness

1. Harvey Cox, "Suggestion of the Devil," "The Powers of Evil," *The New York Times Book Review,* Oct. 19, 1975, p. 8.

2. Ricoeur, *Symbolism of Evil,* p. 76.

3. Laing, *Politics of Experience,* p. 3.

4. Kaufman, *Nietzsche,* p. 25.

5. Laing, *Politics of Experience,* p. 99.

6. Owen Barfield, *Speaker's Meaning* (Wesleyan University Press, 1967), pp. 31, 33.

7. *Ibid.,* p. 44.

8. *Ibid.,* p. 45.

9. *Ibid.,* pp. 69–71.

10. Thomas Kuhn, *Structure of Scientific Revolution* (The University of Chicago Press, 1970), p. 6.

11. L. L. Whyte, *The Unconscious Before Freud* (Basic Books, Inc., 1960), p. 19.

12. Laing, *Politics of Experience,* pp. 98–100.

13. Martin Buber, "Distance and Relation," *Psychiatry,* Vol. 20, No. 2 (1957), pp. 97–104.

14. Owen Barfield, *Saving the Appearances: A Study in Idolatry* (London: Faber & Faber, Ltd., 1957), p. 133.

15. Whyte, *The Unconscious Before Freud,* p. 28.

16. Barfield, *Saving the Appearances,* pp. 126–127.

17. Owen Barfield, *History in English Words* (Wm. B. Eerdmans Publishing Company, 1967), p. 172.

18. Jacobus Sprenger and Heinrich Kramer, *Malleus Maleficarum* (1489), tr. by Montague Summers (London: Folio Society, Ltd., 1968).

19. Barfield, *Speaker's Meaning,* p. 77.

20. George Rosen, *Madness in Society* (The University of Chicago Press, 1968), p. 59.

21. Michel Foucault, *Madness and Civilization* (Pantheon Books, 1965), p. xii.

22. Rosen, *Madness in Society,* p. 6.

23. Paul Tillich, *The Courage to Be* (Yale University Press, 1952), p. 48.

24. *Ibid.,* p. 57.

25. Foucault, *Madness and Civilization,* p. 18.

26. Johan Huizinga in Kathleen Williams (ed.), *Twentieth Century Interpretations of The Praise of Folly* (Prentice-Hall, Inc., 1969), p. 65.

27. Rosen, *Madness in Society,* p. 57.

28. Foucault, *Madness and Civilization,* p. 247.

29. *Ibid.,* p. 264.

30. *Ibid.,* pp. 196–197.

31. *Ibid.,* pp. 219–220.

32. Laing, *Politics of Experience,* p. 96.

33. *Ibid.,* pp. 48–49.

34. Laing, *Divided Self,* p. 12.

Chapter 5. NEITHER SIN NOR MADNESS: EASTERN EQUIVALENTS

1. Heinrich Zimmer, *Philosophies of India,* ed. by Joseph Campbell (Bollingen Series XXVI, Princeton University Press, 1969), p. 4.

2. Thomas Merton, *Zen and the Birds of Appetite* (New Directions, 1968), p. 82.

3. T. S. Eliot, "Burnt Norton," *Four Quartets* (Harcourt, Brace and Company, Inc., 1943), p. 3.

4. It is not possible at this point adequately to elaborate the complex differences in ontology, anthropology, and epistemology between Eastern and Western thought. Very briefly, however, for clarification here, it can be said that generally in the Western tradition man is considered to be radically disjunct from his Source. That is, there is an "infinite distance" between man and God. Man's existential predicament is seen as a broken relationship with his Source, from which he falls into self-idolatry—pride. In Hindu thought man's essential nature is understood to be in harmony with cosmic reality. In Theravada Buddhism, man is viewed as *anatta,* or without self. The root of his suffering is clinging to a desiring empirical ego. His existential predicament is seen as ignorance of his identity with Reality. In the Western mode

of self-understanding, the way out of the predicament is for man to ally himself with the *will* of God and so to transcend his eogcentricity. The possibility of the restoration of the broken relationship lies in the dialogue between man and God, in the medium of history. In Hinduism, man's task is to become aware of his natural identity with cosmic reality and thereby to transcend his encapsulated individual self. In Buddhism, to be released from one's phenomenal self is the goal. In either Eastern or Western view, it is the wall of the enclosed self that must be scaled.

5. This is true in general of the Biblical religious tradition although the mystics, seeking reunion, would be an exception. In the context of this chapter, to avoid confusion with Buddhist terms, I want to note that "separation" always refers to separation from source and "attachment" refers to relatedness to it. In Buddhist thought generally it is "attachment" to the empirical self and world that is to be overcome.

6. "Hinduism" spans a period from approximately 3000 B.C. to the present day.

7. Stuart, *Narcissus,* p. 45.

8. Henri and H. A. Frankfort; John Wilson; and Thorkild Jacobsen, *Before Philosophy* (Penguin Books, Inc., 1972), p. 36.

9. *Mandukya Upanishad,* 7; in the Harper Torchbook edition, 1962, ed. by Swami Nikhilawanda, see p. 165.

10. This is true also of later Hindu thought. In the *Bhagavad Gita* the god Krishna urges that one must dissolve self-concern of the ego so as to discover the Self.

11. In the Hindu view we are, in fact, already liberated, if we would but know it. In a similar way, one who does not know the place of a hidden treasure fails to discover it even though it is directly at hand. So we fail to find the world of Brahman. We find this perspective in regard to seeking the self in the thought of Plato, Augustine, Heidegger, and even in Kierkegaard's statement that the self is "a movement at the spot." It is tempting also to note a connection between Hindu thought and that of Immanuel Kant in the distinction between the "thing in itself" and its "appearance," although for Kant the former is inaccessible to man.

12. Zimmer, *Philosophies of India,* p. 309.

13. Thomas Berry, *Religions of India: Hinduism, Yoga, Buddhism* (Bruce Publishing Company, 1971), p. 82.

14. Zimmer, *Philosophies of India,* p. 464.

15. E. A. Burtt (ed.), *The Teachings of the Compassionate Buddha* (The New American Library of World Literature, Inc., Mentor Religious Classics, 1955), p. 30.

16. Merton, *Zen and the Birds of Appetite,* p. 119.

17. Daisetz Suzuki, "Knowledge and Innocence" in Merton, *ibid.,* p. 107.

18. Merton, *Zen and the Birds of Appetite,* p. 141.

19. Erich Fromm; D. T. Suzuki; and Richard Demartino, *Zen Buddhism and Psychoanalysis* (Harper & Brothers, Colophon Books, 1960), pp. 46–47.

20. *Ibid.,* p. 47.

21. *Ibid.,* pp. 11–12.

22. Merton, *Zen and the Birds of Appetite,* p. 6.

23. Fromm, Suzuki, and Demartino, *Zen Buddhism and Psychoanalysis,* p. 20.

24. *Ibid.,* p. 30.

25. *Ibid.,* p. 31.

26. *Ibid.*

27. *Ibid.*

28. *Ibid.,* p. 56.

29. James Legge, *The Chinese Classics,* Vol. I (Hong Kong; London: Trubner & Co., 1860).

30. *Ibid.*

31. *Ibid.,* 4:25.

32. William Theodore De Bary and the Conference on Ming Thought, *Self and Society in Ming Thought* (Columbia University Press, 1970), p. 15.

33. *Ibid.,* p. 14.

34. Fung Yu-lan, *Spirit of Chinese Philosophy,* tr. by E. R. Hughes (Beacon Press, Inc., 1962), p. 2.

35. Donald J. Munro, *The Concept of Man in Early China* (Stanford University Press, 1969), p. 90. See also Chapter 4.

36. *Ibid.,* p. 155.

37. Herbert Fingarette, *Confucius: The Secular as Sacred* (Harper & Row, Publishers, Inc., Harper Torchbooks, 1972), p. 79; the numerical reference in the text is to the Analects.

38. Fung Yu-lan, *Spirit of Chinese Philosophy,* p. 2.

39. Lao Tzu, *Tao Te Ching,* tr. with an intro. by D. C. Lau (Penguin Books, Inc., 1963).

40. *Ibid.*

41. Munro, *Concept of Man in Early China,* p. 130.

42. Lao Tzu, *Tao Te Ching.*

43. *Ibid.,* VII 19, 19a.

44. Fung Yu-lan, *A Short History of Chinese Philosophy,* ed. by Derk Bodde (The Free Press, 1948), p. 6.

45. Fung Yu-lan, *Spirit of Chinese Philosophy,* p. 6.

Chapter 6. NARCISSISM RECONSIDERED: THE PSYCHOANALYTIC APPROACH

1. Erich Heller, "Observations on Psychoanalysis and Modern Literature," *Salmagundi,* #31–32 (Fall 1975–Winter 1976), p. 17.

2. T. S. Eliot, *The Cocktail Party,* in *The Complete Poems and Plays, 1909–1950* (Harcourt, Brace and Company, Inc., 1952), p. 362.

3. Fromm, Suzuki, and Demartino, *Zen Buddhism and Psychoanalysis,* p. 81.

4. Michel Foucault, *The Order of Things* (Pantheon Books, 1970), p. 373.

5. Paul Tillich, *Theology of Culture,* ed. by Robert C. Kimball (Oxford University Press, 1959), Ch. VIII, especially pp. 123–124. For an expression of a way in which a psychoanalytic model of man can inform the theological model of man, see also Fred Berthold, Jr., "Theology and Self-Understanding," in Peter Homans (ed.), *The Dialogue Between Theology and Psychology* (The University of Chicago Press, 1968).

6. Sigmund Freud, *Collected Papers,* tr. by Joan Riviere, ed. by Ernest Jones (Basic Books, Inc., 1959), Vol. 4, "On Narcissism," p. 30.

7. Freud, *A General Introduction to Psychoanalysis,* p. 423. The following quotations are from pp. 422–428.

8. Freud, *Collected Papers,* Vol. 4, p. 43.

9. *Ibid.*

10. *Ibid.,* p. 42. As George Steiner points out, "Love is a forced remedy"; see his *In Bluebeard's Castle: Some Notes Towards the Redefinition of Culture* (Yale University Press, 1971), p. 52.

11. *Ibid.,* p. 39.

12. Freud, *A General Introduction to Psychoanalysis,* p. 428.

13. Freud, *The Ego and the Id,* tr. by Joan Riviere, ed. by James Strachey (W. W. Norton & Company, Inc., 1961), p. 44.

14. Freud, *Collected Papers,* Vol. 4, pp. 161–162.

15. *Ibid.,* p. 162.

16. *Ibid.*

17. Freud, *The Ego and the Id,* p. 48.

18. Sigmund Freud, *The Complete Psychological Works,* Vol. XX, tr. under general ed. of James Strachey, with Anna Freud (London: The Hogarth Press, Ltd., 1959), p. 168.

19. *Ibid.,* p. 136.

20. Freud, *The Ego and the Id,* p. 48.

21. Freud, *A General Introduction to Psychoanalysis,* p. 431.

22. Stuart, *Narcissus,* p. 122.

23. The primary needs of the infant are described variously as: fundamental body needs by Anna Freud; oral needs by Melanie Klein; need for physical contact, or presence, according to Donald Winnicott; need for contact with the mother, Marguerite Ribble; oral needs on which basic trust is based, Erik Erikson; René Spitz, the need for food; H. Stack Sullivan, the need for tenderness; oral needs—for Ronald Fairbairn; for elaboration of this there is an excellent article by John Bowlby, "The Nature of the Child's Tie to His Mother," in the *International Journal of Psychoanalysis,* 34 (1958), pp. 355–372. I would add Gregory Bateson's view, stated in an *Ecology of Mind*

(especially pp. 201–308), that implies the need for consistently clear and unified communications of one "logical type."

24. Marguerite Ribble, *The Rights of Infants* (Columbia University Press, 1960).

25. Melanie Klein and Joan Riviere (eds.), *Love, Hate and Reparation* (W. W. Norton & Company, Inc., 1964), p. 21.

26. Melanie Klein, "Mourning and Its Relations to Manic-Depressive States," in *Contributions to Psychoanalysis 1921–1945* with an intro. by Ernest Jones (London: The Hogarth Press, Ltd., 1950), p. 314.

27. Ribble, *The Rights of Infants*, p. 9.

28. Freud, *Collected Papers*, Vol. 4, p. 49.

29. For further information on the post-Freudian development of psychoanalytic thought, see the Related Readings here (Brown, Robinson, Ruitenbeek).

30. Klein, "A Contribution to the Psychogenesis of Manic-Depressive States," in *Contributions to Psychoanalysis 1921–1945*.

31. W. Ronald D. Fairbairn, *An Object-Relations Theory of the Personality* (Basic Books, Inc., 1954), p. 31. Among other members of the "object relations" school of thought are Harry Guntrip and Donald Winnicott.

32. *Ibid.*, p. 49.

33. *Ibid.*, p. 55.

34. *Ibid.*, pp. 56–57 (1941). Note also Donald Winnicott's view on the origins of disturbance in the infant-mother relationship, especially his concept of the "good-enough" mother. He points to schizoid introversion as both an effort to protect the love object from the infant's destructive need, his "ruthless love," as well as to protect the infant from the impingement of the disturbing external object.

35. *Ibid.*, p. 7 (1940).

36. *Ibid.*, p. 101.

37. *Ibid.*, pp. 103–115.

38. *Ibid.*, p. 108.

39. *Ibid.*

40. Stuart, *Narcissus*, p. 59.

41. Fairbairn, *An Object-Relations Theory of the Personality*, p. 26.

42. Hyman Spotnitz, *Modern Psychoanalysis of the Schizophrenic Patient* (Grune & Stratton, Inc., 1969), p. 18.

43. Narcissism has in recent years become the subject of intensive research; for a background context of the modern psychoanalytic theory developed by Dr. Spotnitz and his associates, see references in the Related Readings to Rado, Lorand, Nunberg, Reich, Reik, Ehrenwald, Polatin; for a selection of articles by his associates, see the Related Readings for this chapter: Bloch, Clevans, Davis, Love, Nelson; for other views on narcissism, see references in the Related Readings to Kernberg and Kohut, and in Ch. 1, note 13, above, to Lester Schwartz. The etiology of the disorder is complex

and its origin is not attributed to either constitutional or environmental factors exclusively, but rather to the relationship between the infant and its environment. It is not understood as a disease lodged in the individual but as the individual's response to its original matrix. For related nonpsychoanalytic views, see Lewis Thomas, *Lives of a Cell*, and Bateson, *Steps to an Ecology of Mind* (Ch. 3, note 33, above).

44. Donald Winnicott, *Collected Papers* (London: Tavistock Publications, Ltd., 1958), p. 279.

45. Harry Guntrip, *Schizoid Phenomena, Object Relations and the Self* (International Universities Press, Inc., 1969), p. 358.

46. Spotnitz, "A Preanalytic Technique," p. 193.

47. Spotnitz, *Modern Psychoanalysis*, p. 8.

48. *Ibid.*, p. 11.

49. Spotnitz, "A Preanalytic Technique," p. 194. There seems to be a consensus among such diverse figures as Melanie Klein, Ronald Fairbairn, Donald Winnicott, Otto Kernberg, on the centrality of aggression in narcissism. George Steiner states (see note 10) that "it is . . . notable that the theory of personality, as it develops from Hegel to Nietzsche and Freud . . . is essentially a theory of aggression."

50. Hyman Spotnitz, "Techniques for the Resolution of the Narcissistic Defense," in *Psychoanalytic Techniques,* ed. by Benjamin Wolman (Basic Books, Inc., 1967), p. 275.

51. Spotnitz, *Modern Psychoanalysis*, p. 37.

52. *Ibid.*, p. 39; and cf. Winnicott, *Collected Papers*, "Hate in the Counter-Transference."

53. Following the analysis in Hyman Spotnitz, "The Narcissistic Defense in Schizophrenia," in *Clinical Approaches to Schizophrenia,* March 1961, p. 32, Monograph of the Psychology Department of the Stuyvesant Polyclinic, New York City. For a different viewpoint, see Carl Rogers (ed.), *The Therapeutic Relationship and Its Impact* (University of Wisconsin Press, 1967), esp. pp. 97 ff.

54. Spotnitz, "Resolution," p. 275.

55. Spotnitz, "Narcissistic Defense," p. 32.

56. *Ibid.*

57. See Erich Fromm, *The Crisis of Psychoanalysis* (Fawcett Publications, Inc., 1970), p. 41; Rollo May, *Love and Will* (W. W. Norton & Company, Inc., 1969); Ronald Fairbairn, *An Object-Relations Theory of the Personality,* as in note 31.

58. Hyman Spotnitz, "Insulation and Immunization in Schizophrenia," in *Reports in Medical and Clinical Psychology* (Stuyvesant Polyclinic, 1963), p. 18.

59. Spotnitz, "Preanalytic Technique," p. 193.

60. Spotnitz, "Narcissistic Defense," p. 33; the important question of countertransference is not being dealt with here, however, cf. Spotnitz,

Modern Psychoanalysis, pp. 155–177, and Winnicott, *Collected Papers,* cited in note 52.

61. *Ibid.*

62. See Spotnitz, "Preanalytic Technique," p. 195, and "Strengthening the Ego Through the Release of Frustration Aggression," *American Journal of Orthopsychiatry,* Vol. XXVIII, #4 (Oct. 1958), pp. 796–798, for the following discussion.

63. Fairbairn, *An Object-Relations Theory of the Personality,* p. 7.

64. Fromm, *Crisis in Psychoanalysis,* p. 41.

65. Ernest Becker, *The Denial of Death,* pp. 218–219.

66. *Ibid.,* p. 198.

67. *Ibid.*

68. Phillip Rieff, *Freud: Mind of a Moralist* (Doubleday & Company, Inc., Anchor Books, 1961), p. 391.

69. Gregory Bateson and Juergen Ruesch, *Communication* (W. W. Norton & Company, Inc., 1968).

Chapter 7. RESOLUTION

1. Herbert Fingarette, *The Self in Transformation* (Harper & Row, Publishers, Inc., Harper Torchbooks, 1963), p. 9.

2. Kierkegaard, *Point of View,* p. 40.

3. Kierkegaard, *Training in Christianity,* p. 132.

4. See, for instance, Marie Coleman Nelson (ed.), *Roles and Paradigms in Psychotherapy* (Grune & Stratton, Inc., 1968).

5. Spotnitz, *Modern Psychoanalysis,* p. 206.

6. Alan Watts, *Psychotherapy East and West* (The New American Library of World Literature, Inc., Mentor Books, 1963), p. 28.

7. Barfield, *Saving the Appearances,* Ch. XX.

8. Suzuki, Fromm, and Demartino, *Zen Buddhism and Psychoanalysis,* p. 94.

9. *Ibid.,* p. 120 and p. 96.

10. It seems as though it is only the exceptional few who have been able successfully to deal with the disturbance at the Source which plagues us all and threatens mankind with further violence and destructiveness. The few I refer to are represented in Western religious literature by those who could contend with God, for instance, by Pascal, who possessed the extraordinary belief that "God is more abominable than I" (Payne, *Hubris, A Study of Pride,* p. 210), and St. Theresa of Avila, who when she enters the dark night of the soul wonders at God's incessant and ferocious cruelty *(ibid.).* Job and Luther are among those who have contended with God and as a consequence have undergone a transformation—a rebirth. Such a transformation or rebirth is the mark of the sages and is the core and source of their wisdom.

Related Readings

Preface

Guénon, René, *The Crisis of the Modern World,* tr. by Marco Pallis and Richard Nicholson. London: Luzac and Company, Ltd., 1962.

Hopper, Stanley Romaine, *The Crisis of Faith.* Abingdon-Cokesbury Press, 1944.

Slater, Philip, *The Pursuit of Loneliness.* Beacon Press, Inc., 1970.

Chapter 1. Narcissus Reconsidered: The Myth

Bachelard, Gaston, *The Psychoanalysis of Fire,* tr. by Alan C. Ross. Preface by Northrop Frye. Beacon Press, Inc., 1964.

Campbell, Joseph, *The Flight of the Wild Gander.* The Viking Press, Inc., 1969.

Cassirer, Ernst, *Language and Myth,* tr. by Susanne K. Langer. Dover Publications, Inc., 1946.

Deutsch, Helene, *A Psychoanalytic Study of the Myth of Dionysus and Apollo.* International Universities Press, Inc., 1969.

Eliade, Mircea, *Images and Symbols,* tr. by Philip Mairet. Sheed & Ward, Inc., 1969.

Fitch, Elliot Robert, *Odyssey of the Self-Centered Self.* London: George Allen & Unwin, Ltd., 1962.

Ibsen, Henrik, *Peer Gynt,* tr. by Michael Meyner. Doubleday & Company, Inc., Anchor Books, 1963.

Lavelle, Louis, *The Dilemma of Narcissus,* tr. by W. T. Gairdner. London: George Allen & Unwin, Ltd., 1973.

Leach, Edmund, *Genesis as Myth.* London: Jonathan Cape, Ltd., 1969.

Malcolm, Henry, *Generation of Narcissus.* Little, Brown & Company, 1971.

Rank, Otto, *Myth of the Birth of the Hero: A Psychological Interpretation of Mythology.* Nervous and Mental Disease Monographs, No. 8, 1914.

Slater, Philip, *The Glory of Hera.* Beacon Press, Inc., 1971.

Chapter 2. Sin: The Flight from the Self

Augustinus, St. Aurelius, *The Confessions of St. Augustine,* tr. by John K. Ryan. Doubleday & Company, Inc., Image Books, 1962.

Bonifazi, Conrad, *Christendom Attacked: A Comparison of Kierkegaard and Nietzsche.* London: Rockliff Publishing Corporation, 1953.

Brunner, Emil, *Man in Revolt.* The Westminster Press, 1947.

Buber, Martin, *I and Thou,* tr. by R. G. Smith. Charles Scribner's Sons, 1958.

Diem, Hermann, *Kierkegaard's Dialectic of Existence,* tr. by Harold Knight. Edinburgh: Oliver & Boyd, Ltd., 1959.

Dostoevsky, Feodor, *The Double.* Indiana University Press, 1966.

———*Notes from the Underground.* Dell Publishing Co., Inc., 1967.

Farber, Leslie, *The Ways of the Will.* Basic Books, Inc., 1966.

Friedman, Maurice, *To Deny Our Nothingness.* Dell Publishing Co., Inc., 1967.

Harper, Ralph, *The Seventh Solitude: Man's Isolation in Kierkegaard, Dostoevsky, and Nietzsche.* The Johns Hopkins Press, 1965.

Herberg, Will, *Judaism and Modern Man.* Meridian Books, Inc., 1956.

Hubben, William, *Dostoevsky, Kierkegaard, Nietzsche, and Kafka.* Collier Books, 1966.

Ignatius de Loyola, St., *The Spiritual Exercises of St. Ignatius,* tr. by Anthony Mottola. Introduction by Robert W. Gleason. Doubleday & Company, Inc., Image Books, 1964.

Kaufman, Walter (ed.), *Existentialism from Dostoevsky to Sartre.* New American Library, Meridian Books, 1962.

Kierkegaard, Søren, *Repetition: An Essay in Experimental Psychology* (1843), tr. by Walter Lowrie. Princeton University Press, 1941.

———*Stages on Life's Way* (1845), tr. by Walter Lowrie. Princeton University Press, 1940.

———*The Present Age and Two Ethico-Religious Treatises* (1845 and 1949), tr. by Alexander Dru and Walter Lowrie. London: Oxford University Press, 1940.

———*Purity of Heart* (1847), tr. by Douglas V. Steere. Harper & Brothers, Harper Torchbooks, 1956.

———*The Gospel of Suffering; and, The Lilies of the Field* (1847), tr. by David F. and Lillian Marvin Swenson. Augsburg Publishing House, 1947.

———*Works of Love* (1847), tr. by David F. and Lillian Marvin Swenson. Princeton University Press, 1946.

Lapsley, James N. (ed.), *The Concept of Willing.* Foreword by Seward Hiltner. Abingdon Press, 1967.

Loomis, Earl A., *The Self in Pilgrimage.* Harper & Brothers, 1960.

Miller, L. L., *In Search of the Self: The Individual in the Thought of Kierkegaard.* Muhlenberg Press, 1962.

Moustakas, Clark (ed.), *The Self.* Harper & Brothers, 1956.

Niebuhr, Reinhold, *The Nature and Destiny of Man.* Charles Scribner's Sons, 1949.

Patrick, Denzil G. M., *Pascal and Kierkegaard*, Vols. I and II. London: Lutterworth Press, 1947.

Pelikan, Jaroslav, *From Luther to Kierkegaard*. Concordia Publ. House, 1950.

Plath, Sylvia, *The Bell Jar*. Harper & Row, Publishers, Inc., 1971.

Sarraute, Nathalie, *Portrait of a Man Unknown*. Preface by Jean-Paul Sartre; tr. by Marie Jolas. George Braziller, Inc., 1958.

Sexton, Anne, *Live or Die*. Houghton Mifflin Company, 1966.

Stein, M. R.; White, D. M.; and Vidich, A. J. (eds.), *Identity and Anxiety*. The Free Press of Glencoe, Inc., 1960.

Sypher, F. Wylie, *Loss of the Self in Modern Literature and Art*. Vintage Books, Inc., 1964.

Tillich, Paul, *The Courage to Be*. Yale University Press, 1952.

——*Systematic Theology*, Vols. I–III. The University of Chicago Press, 1959.

Chapter 3. MADNESS: THE DIVIDED SELF

Baudelaire, Charles, *Flowers of Evil*, tr. and ed. by Marthiel and Jackson Mathews. New Directions, 1955.

Binswanger, Ludwig, *Being-in-the-World*, tr. by Jacob Needleman. Basic Books, Inc., 1963.

Boss, Medard, *Psychoanalysis and Daseinanalysis*, tr. by Ludwig B. Lefebre. Basic Books, Inc., 1963.

Boyers, Robert, and Orrill, Robert, *R. D. Laing, and Anti-Psychiatry*. Harper & Row, Publishers, Inc., 1971.

Chesler, Phyllis, *Women and Madness*. Doubleday & Company, Inc., 1972.

Cooper, David, *Psychiatry and Anti-Psychiatry*. London: Tavistock Publications, Ltd., 1967.

Dabrowski, Kazimierz, *Positive Disintegration*, ed. by Jason Aronson. Little, Brown & Company, 1964.

Friedenberg, Edgar Z., *R. D. Laing*. The Viking Press, Inc., 1973.

Frondizi, Risieri, *The Nature of the Self*. Yale University Press, 1953.

Goffman, Erving, *Asylums*. Doubleday & Company, Inc., 1961.

Henry, Jules, *Culture Against Man*. Vintage Books, Inc., 1963.

——*Pathways to Madness*. Vintage Books, Inc., 1973.

Jung, Carl, *Aion, Collected Works*, Vol. IX, Part 2. Princeton University Press, 1961.

Kaplan, Bert (ed.), *The Inner World of Mental Illness*. Harper & Row, Publishers, Inc., 1964.

Laing, Ronald D., *Reason and Violence, A Decade of Sartre's Philosophy 1950–1960*. With D. G. Cooper. London: Tavistock Publications, Ltd., 1964.

——"Mystification, Confusion and Conflict" in *Intensive Family Therapy. Theoretical and Practical Aspects*, ed. by Ivan Bszobrmenyi-Nagy and

James L. Framo. Harper & Row, Publishers, Inc., 1965.

————*Interpersonal Perception, A Theory and a Method of Research.* With H. Phillipson and A. R. Lee. London: Tavistock Publications, Ltd., 1966.

————"Family and Individual Structure" in *Predicament of the Family,* ed. by Peter Lomas. International Universities Press, Inc., 1967.

————"The Collusion Function of Pairing in Analytic Groups," *British Journal of Medical Psychology,* Vol. XXXI (1958), pp. 117–123. (With Aaron Esterton.)

————"Ritualization and Abnormal Behavior" in *Ritualization of Behavior in Animals and Man. Philosophical Transactions.* Royal Society of London, Series B, Biological Science, 251 (772): 331–335, 1966.

————*The Politics of the Family.* Vintage Books, Inc., 1972.

————and Esterton, Aaron, *Sanity, Madness and the Family:* Vol. I, *Families of Schizophrenics.* Basic Books, Inc., 1964.

Lyons, Joseph, *Psychology and the Measure of Man: A Phenomenological Approach.* The Free Press of Glencoe, Inc., 1963.

May, Rollo (ed.), *Existential Psychology.* Random House, Inc., 1961.

May, Rollo; Angel, E.; and Ellenberger, H. P. (eds.), *Existence: A New Dimension in Psychiatry and Psychology.* Basic Books, Inc., 1958.

Ruitenbeek, Hendrik (ed.), *Going Crazy: The Radical Therapy of R. D. Laing, and Others.* Bantam Books, Inc., 1972.

Rycroft, Charles (ed.), *Psychoanalysis Observed.* Coward-McCann, Inc., 1967.

Sartre, Jean-Paul, *Critique de la Raison Dialectique.* Paris: Librairie Gallimard, 1960.

————*No Exit and Three Other Plays.* Vintage Books, Inc., 1958.

————*The Transcendence of the Ego,* tr. by Forrest Williams and Robert Kirkpatrick. The Noonday Press, 1957.

Sonneman, Ulrich, *Existence and Therapy: An Introduction to Phenomenological Psychology and Existential Analysis.* Grune & Stratton, Inc., 1954.

Stern, Alfred, *Sartre: His Philosophy and Psychoanalysis.* Liberal Arts Press, Inc., 1953.

Szasz, Thomas S., *The Myth of Mental Illness.* Dell Publishing Co., Inc., 1961.

Tillich, Paul, "Existence and Psychotherapy," *Review of Experimental Psychology* Vol. I, No. 1 (1961).

————"Psychoanalysis, Existentialism and Theology," *Pastoral Psychology,* Vol. 9 (1958), pp. 9–17.

Trilling, Lionel, *The Opposing Self.* The Viking Press, Inc., 1968.

Van den Berg, J. H., *The Phenomenological Approach to Psychiatry.* Charles C Thomas, 1955.

Van Kaam, Adrian, *Existential Foundations of Psychology.* Duquesne University Press, 1966.

Chapter 4. Sin and Madness: A Transformation of Consciousness

Bateson, Gregory, and Mead, Margaret, *Balinese Character.* New York Academy of Science, 1942.

Benedict, Ruth, *Patterns of Culture.* Houghton Mifflin Company, 1934.

Brown, Norman O., *Life Against Death: The Psychoanalytic Meaning of History.* Random House, Inc., 1959.

Cornford, Francis M., *From Religion to Philosophy.* Harper & Brothers, Harper Torchbooks, 1957.

Dostoevsky, Feodor, *The Possessed.* Random House, Inc., 1963.

Huxley, Aldous, *The Devils of Loudun.* Harper & Row, Publishers, Inc., 1971.

Jaspers, Karl, *General Psychopathology,* tr. by J. Hoenig and Marian W. Hamilton. The University of Chicago Press, 1963.

John of the Cross, St., *Dark Night of the Soul,* tr. and ed. by E. Allison Peers. Doubleday & Company, Inc., Image Books, Inc., 1959.

Menninger, Karl, *Whatever Became of Sin?* Hawthorne Bks., Inc., 1973.

Ornstein, Robert E., *The Psychology of Consciousness.* W. H. Freeman and Company, 1972.

Teilhard de Chardin, Pierre, *The Divine Milieu.* Harper & Brothers, 1960.

Thompson, William Irwin, *At the Edge of History.* Harper & Row, Publishers, Inc., 1971.

Chapter 5. Neither Sin nor Madness: Eastern Equivalents

Altizer, Thomas J. J., *Oriental Mysticism and Biblical Eschatology.* The Westminster Press, 1961.

Barrett, William (ed.), *Zen Buddhism: Selected Writings by D. T. Suzuki.* Doubleday & Company, Inc., Anchor Books, 1956.

Bucke, Richard Maurice, *Cosmic Consciousness.* University Books, Inc., 1961.

Burtt, Edwin A. (ed.), *The Teachings of the Compassionate Buddha.* New American Library, Mentor Books, 1955.

Ch'en, Kenneth, *Buddhism in China.* Princeton University Press, 1964.

Creel, H. G., *Chinese Thought, from Confucius to Mao Tze Tung.* New American Library, Mentor Books, 1953.

Conze, Edward (ed.), *Buddhist Texts Through the Ages.* Harper & Row, Publishers, Inc., Harper Torchbooks, 1964.

De Bary, William Theodore (ed.), *Sources of Indian Tradition,* Vol. I. Columbia University Press, 1958.

———(ed.), *Sources of Chinese Tradition.* Columbia University Press, 1960.

Dunne, John S., *The Way of All the Earth.* The Macmillan Company, 1972.

Edwardes, Michael, *East-West Passage.* Taplinger Publishing Co., Inc., 1971.

Govinda, Lama Anagraika, *The Psychological Attitude of Early Buddhist Philosophy.* Samuel Weiser, Inc., 1974.

Herrigel, Eugen, *Zen in the Art of Archery.* Introduction by D. T. Suzuki, tr. by R. F. C. Hull. Vintage Books, Inc., 1971.

Humphreys, Christmas, *Buddhism.* Penguin Books, Inc., 1971.

The I Ching, ed. by Max Müller and tr. by James Legge, Vol. XVI, Sacred Books of the East. Dover Publications, Inc., 1963.

Isherwood, Christopher (ed.), *Vedanta for Modern Man.* Harper & Brothers, 1951.

Jacobs, Hans, *Western Psychotherapy and Hindu Sâdhanâ.* International Universities Press, Inc., 1961.

James, William, *The Varieties of Religious Experience.* Collier Books, 1961.

Lao Tzu, *Treastise on Response and Retribution,* tr. by D. T. Suzuki and Paul Carus. The Open Court Publishing Co., 1973.

Legge, James (tr. and ed.), *The Texts of Taoism.* Dover Publications, Inc., 1962.

Luk, Charles, *The Secrets of Chinese Meditation.* London: Rider & Co., 1964.

Murphy, Gardner, and Murphy, Lois B. (eds.), *Asian Psychology.* Basic Books, Inc., 1968.

Needham, Joseph, *Within the Four Seas: The Dialogue of East and West.* London: George Allen & Unwin, Ltd., 1969.

Northrop, F. S. C., *The Meeting of East and West.* The Macmillan Company, Collier Books, 1946.

Radhakrishnan, Sarvepalli, and Moore, Charles, *A Source Book in Indian Philosophy.* Princeton University Press, 1957.

————and Raju, P. T., *The Concept of Man.* Johnsen Publishing Company, 1960.

Smith, Huston, *The Religions of Man.* Harper & Brothers, Perennial Library, 1958.

Suzuki, D. T., *Essays in Zen Buddhism.* Harper & Brothers, 1949.

Waley, Arthur (ed. and tr.), *The Way and Its Power.* Grove Press, Inc., 1958.

Weber, Max, *The Religion of China.* Free Press, 1951.

Welch, Holmes, *Taoism.* Beacon Press, Inc., 1972.

Yang, Ch'ing k'un, *Religion in Chinese Society.* University of California Press, 1961.

Zaehner, R. G., *Zen, Drugs and Mysticism.* Pantheon Books, 1972.

Chapter 6. NARCISSISM RECONSIDERED: THE PSYCHOANALYTIC APPROACH

Abenheimer, Karl M., "On Narcissism—Including an Analysis of Shakespeare's King Lear," *British Journal of Medical Psychology,* Vol. XXX (1957), pp. 322–329.

Arieti, Silvano, *Interpretation of Schizophrenia.* Robert Brunner, Inc., 1955.

Bach, George, and Wyden, Peter, *The Intimate Enemy.* Avon Books, 1972.

Bakan, David, *Disease, Pain and Sacrifice.* The University of Chicago Press, 1968.

Balint, Michael, *The Basic Fault.* London: Tavistock Publications, Ltd., 1968.

Bloch, Dorothy, "Feelings That Kill: The Effect of the Wish for Infanticide in Neurotic Depression," *Psychoanalytic Review,* Vol. LII (1965), pp. 51–66.

Bowlby, John, *Attachment and Loss,* Vol. I, *Attachment;* Vol. II, *Separation.* Basic Books, Inc., 1973.

Brown, J. A. C., *Freud and the Post-Freudians.* Penguin Books, Inc., 1969.

Clevans, Ethel, "The Fear of a Schizophrenic Man," *Psychoanalysis,* Vol. V, No. 4 (1957), pp. 58–67.

Davis, Harold, "Short-term Psychoanalytic Therapy with Hospitalized Schizophrenics," *Psychoanalytic Review,* Vol. LII (1965–1966), pp. 421–488.

Dollard, John; Doob, Leonard W.; Miller, Neal E.; Mowrer, O. H.; and Sears, Robert, *Frustration and Aggression.* Yale University Press, 1939.

Ehrenwald, Jan, *Neurosis in the Family and Patterns of Psychosocial Defense.* Harper & Row, Publishers, Inc., 1963.

Eissler, Ruth; Freud, Anna; Hartmann, Heinz, Kris, Ernst (eds.), *The Psychoanalytic Study of the Child,* Vols. III, IV, V, XXIII. International Universities Press, Inc., 1945–1975.

English, Spurgeon O., and Pearson, G. H. J., *Emotional Problems of Living.* W. W. Norton & Company, Inc., 1963.

Erikson, Erik H., *Childhood and Society.* W. W. Norton & Company, Inc., 1963.

——*Identity and the Life Cycle.* International Universities Press, Inc. 1968.

Federn, Paul, "Narcissism in the Structure of the Ego," *The International Journal of Psychoanalysis,* Vol. IX (Oct. 1928), Pt. 4.

Fenichel, Otto, *The Psychoanalytic Theory of the Neurosis.* W. W. Norton & Company, Inc., 1945.

Ferenczi, Sandor, *Thalassa, A Theory of Genitality,* tr. by H. A. Bunker. The Psychoanalytic Quarterly, Inc., 1938.

Flugel, J. C., *The Psychoanalytic Study of the Family.* London: The Hogarth Press, Ltd., 1966.

Freud, Sigmund, *Civilization and Its Discontents,* tr. and ed. by James Strachey. W. W. Norton & Company, Inc., 1962.

——and Pfister, Oskar R., *Psychoanalysis and Faith,* ed. by H. Meng and E. L. Freud. Basic Books, Inc., 1963.

Fromm, Erich, *The Anatomy of Human Destructiveness.* Holt, Rinehart, & Winston, Inc., 1973.

Fromm-Reichmann, Frieda, *Principles of Intensive Psychotherapy.* The University of Chicago Press, 1955.

Gendlin, Eugene, *Experiencing and the Creation of Meaning.* The Free Press of Glencoe, Inc., 1962.

Greenson, Ralph, *The Technique and Practice of Psychoanalysis.* International Universities Press, Inc., 1967.

Guntrip, Harry, *Personality Structure and Human Interaction.* International Universities Press, Inc., 1961.

———*Psychoanalytic Theory, Therapy, and the Self.* Basic Books, Inc., 1971.

Jacobson, Edith, *Depression.* International Universities Press, Inc., 1971.

———*The Self and The Object World.* International Universities Press, Inc., 1964.

Jung, Carl G., *The Integration of the Personality,* tr. by Stanley Dell. London: Routledge & Kegan Paul, Ltd., 1956.

Kernberg, Otto, *Borderline Conditions and Pathological Narcissism.* Jason Aronson, Inc., 1975.

Klein, Melanie; Heimann, Paula; Isaacs, Susan; and Riviere, Joan (eds.), *Developments in Psychoanalysis.* London: The Hogarth Press, Ltd., 1952.

Kohut, Heinz, *Analysis of the Self: A Systematic Approach to the Psychoanalytic Treatment of Narcissistic Personality Disorders.* International Universities Press, Inc., 1971.

Lorand, Sandor, *Techniques of Psychoanalytic Therapy.* International Universities Press, Inc., 1946.

Lorenz, Konrad, *On Aggression.* Harcourt, Brace and World, Inc., 1963.

Love, Sidney, and Feldman, Yonata, "The Disguised Cry for Help: Narcissistic Mothers and Their Children," in *Psychoanalytic Review,* Vol. XLVIII, No. 2 (1961), pp. 1–16.

Mahler, Margaret S.; Pine, Fred; and Bergman, Anni, *Symbiosis and Individuation.* Basic Books, Inc., 1976.

Nelson, Benjamin (ed.), *Freud and the Twentieth Century.* Meridian Books, Inc., 1963.

Nelson, Marie C., "Externalization of the Toxic Introject," *Psychoanalytic Review,* Vol. XLIII, No. 2 (1956), pp. 235–242.

Nunberg, Herman, *Principles of Psychoanalysis.* International Universities Press, Inc., 1955.

Piaget, Jean, *The Child and Reality.* Grossman Publishers, 1973.

Polatin, Philip, *A Guide to Treatment in Psychiatry.* J. B. Lippincott Company, 1966.

Rado, Sandor, *Psychoanalysis of Behavior.* Grune & Stratton, Inc., Vol. I, 1956; Vol. II, 1962.

Reich, Wilhelm, *Character Analysis.* Farrar, Straus & Giroux, Inc., 1972.

Reik, Theodor, *Listening with the Third Ear.* Farrar, Straus & Company, Inc., 1948.

Robinson, Paul A., *The Freudian Left: Wilhelm Reich, Géza Róheim, Herbert Marcuse.* Harper & Row, Publishers, Inc., 1969.

Róheim, Géza, *Magic and Schizophrenia,* ed. by Warner Munsterberger. Foreword by Sandor Lorand. Indiana University Press, 1970
———*Psychoanalysis and Anthropology.* International Universities Press, Inc., 1950.
Rosen, John N., *Psychoanalysis Direct and Indirect.* The Doylestown Foundation, 1964.
Ruitenbeek, Hendrik M., *Heirs to Freud.* Grove Press, Inc., 1966.
———(ed.), *Psychoanalysis and Existential Philosophy.* E. P. Dutton & Co., Inc., 1962.
Searles, Harold, *Collected Papers on Schizophrenia and Related Subjects.* International Universities Press, Inc., 1965.
Sèchehaye, Marguerite A., *Symbolic Realization,* tr. by Barbrö Würsten and Helmut Würsten. International Universities Press, Inc., 1952.
———*Autobiography of a Schizophrenic Girl,* tr. by Grace Rubin-Rabson. Grune & Stratton, Inc., 1965.
Spitz, René, *The First Year of Life.* International Universities Press, Inc., 1965.
———*No and Yes: On the Genesis of Human Communication.* International Universities Press, Inc., 1957.
Spotnitz, Hyman, and Meadow, Phyllis W., *Treatment of the Narcissistic Neuroses.* Manhattan Center for Advanced Psychoanalytic Studies, 1976.
Storr, Anthony, *Human Aggression.* Bantam Books, Inc., 1968.
Sullivan, Charles T., *Freud and Fairbairn: Two Theories of Ego Psychology.* Preface by W. Ronald D. Fairbairn. The Doylestown Foundation, 1963.
Sullivan, Harry Stack, *Schizophrenia as a Human Process.* W. W. Norton and Company, Inc., 1962.
Suttie, Ian D., *The Origins of Love and Hate.* The Julian Press, Inc., 1952.
Winnicott, Donald W., *The Family and Individual Development.* Basic Books, Inc., 1965.
———*The Maturational Processes and the Facilitating Environment.* International Universities Press, Inc., 1965.
Wolman, Benjamin B. (ed.), *Psychoanalytic Techniques.* Basic Books, Inc., 1967.

Chapter 7. RESOLUTION

Boyers, Robert (ed.), *Psychological Man: Approaches to an Emergent Social Type.* Salmagundi, No. 20, Summer-Fall, 1972.
Fromm, Erich, *Psychoanalysis and Religion.* Yale University Press, 1959.
Havens, Joseph *Psychology and Religion.* D. Van Nostrand Company, Inc., 1968.
Homans, Peter, *Theology After Freud.* The Bobbs-Merrill Company, Inc., 1970.

Klineberg, Otto, *The Human Dimension in International Relations.* Holt, Rinehart & Winston, Inc., 1964.

Rank, Otto, *Beyond Psychology.* Dover Publications, Inc., 1941.

Richardson, Herbert, and Cutler, Donald (eds.), *Transcendence.* Beacon Press, Inc., 1969.

Rieff, Philip, *Fellow Teachers.* Harper & Row, Publishers, Inc., 1973.

————*The Triumph of the Therapeutic: Uses of Faith After Freud.* Harper & Row, Publishers, Inc., 1966.

Tillich, Paul, *Theology of Culture,* ed. by Robert C. Kimball. London: Oxford University Press, 1959.

Index